How to...
cook the Weight Watchers way

SWITCH

SIMON & SCHUSTER
A VIACOM COMPANY

Becky Johnson and Joy Skipper

First published in Great Britain by Simon & Schuster UK Ltd, 2005
A Viacom Company

Simon & Schuster UK Ltd, Africa House, 64–78 Kingsway, London WC2B 6AH

Weight Watchers Publications Team: Corrina Griffin, Lucy Davidson, Julia Cook, Nina Bhogal

Photography and styling by Steve Baxter
Food preparation by Carol Tennant
Design by Jane Humphrey
Typesetting by Stylize Digital Artwork Ltd
Printed and bound in China

A CIP catalogue for this book is available from the British Library

ISBN 0 7432 39008

Pictured on the back cover: Bombay popcorn page 18; Roast lamb with mint sauce page 166; Raspberry tart page 190

Recipe notes:
All fruits, vegetables and eggs are medium sized unless otherwise stated.

Raw Eggs: Only the freshest eggs should be used. Pregnant women, the elderly and children should avoid recipes with eggs which are not fully cooked or raw.

Recipe timings are approximate and meant to be guidelines. Please note that the preparation time includes all the steps up to and following the main cooking time(s).

 You'll find this easy to read *POINTS*® value logo on every recipe throughout this book. The logo represents the number of *POINTS* per serving each recipe contains. The easy to use *POINTS* system is designed to help you eat what you want, when you want – as long as you stay within your *POINTS* allowance – giving you the freedom to enjoy the food *you* love.

 You'll find this distinctive **NoCount**™ icon on every recipe that can be followed freely on the **NoCount** food plan. These recipes contain only foods that form part of the **NoCount** food listings – helping you to enjoy the foods you love on your weight loss journey.

Ⓥ This symbol denotes a vegetarian recipe and assumes that, where relevant, free range eggs, vegetarian cheese, vegetarian virtually fat free fromage frais and vegetarian low fat crème fraîche are used. Virtually fat free fromage frais and low fat crème fraîche may contain traces of gelatine so they are not always vegetarian. Please check the labels.

Contents

Lose the weight – not the taste!

People often believe that eating healthily is synonymous with dull dinners, but just because you are watching your weight you don't have to miss out on one of life's **true delights** – delicious food. Whether you are a dab hand in the kitchen or a fast food fanatic there's no need to lose out on tastes and flavours just because you are **switching to a healthier lifestyle**.

And now you won't have to! This fantastic cookbook is packed full of hints and tips showing you how you can **cook the Weight Watchers** way as well as giving you great ideas and **fantastic recipes** to help you make the most of your cooking. Whether you are new to the kitchen or an established cook, this is the cookbook that will teach you how to **make the most** of the huge variety of food and flavours available, whilst still making it possible to lose or maintain your weight.

You'll find **step by step** instructions on how to cook your favourite dishes and numerous tips to help you understand which flavours complement certain foods and bring out the best in them. Look for '**How to**' boxes in which you'll find more basic cooking tips that will give you **maximum flavour** for minimum *POINTS* values.

All these **cooking methods** are easy to follow and once you have mastered them, they'll take you from **strength to strength** in your cooking and your weight loss. You'll be amazed at how easy healthy cooking can be – and it's all so tasty you won't believe that you're actually eating **low-fat alternatives**. We bet your family won't be able to tell the difference either!

The new **Switch**™ programme helps you stay **motivated to lose weight** and still live in the real word. All of this comes down to feeling comfortable with the choices that you make for yourself. Whether you are following **NoCount** or **Full Choice** this cookbook will provide you with the inspiration you need. There are **more than 200 recipes**, half of which are NoCount, with **easy to read *POINTS*** values for each recipe and a distinctive icon for those that are **NoCount**.

The chapters are geared to specific eating situations to help you find just the meal to suit your circumstances. So, whether you are on a budget, cooking for friends or want a fast and fabulous meal after work, you'll find just the chapter and recipes to **suit your situation**.

How to cook the Weight Watchers Way is here to support you on your **weight loss journey** and to help keep you there once you have **succeeded**. It's time to get started on your new way of life and once you know how to cook the Weight Watchers way you'll never want to switch back!

Simply soups

You simply can't beat the comfort and warmth of a homemade soup. It's good for you, will fill you up, and tastes fantastic as well. And if you're following the **Switch** programme you can really use soups to your advantage. There are lots of clever ways to use soups that will help to keep you on the road to success. You can make batches of the zero soups and snack on them throughout the day, use vegetable-packed soups to meet healthy eating recommendations of five portions of vegetables per day or have a bowl of zero vegetable soup before you go out for dinner to stave off hunger pangs and allow you to enjoy your evening without your *POINTS* values running away with you.

Smooth gazpacho (page 11)

[comforting]

French onion soup

 ### Spicy noodle soup

Filling and fabulous – with deliciously cheesy croûtons.

A meal of a soup! Enjoy it as a light lunch or supper dish.

Ⓨ *11½ POINTS values per recipe* takes 50 minutes

Ⓨ *13 POINTS values per recipe* takes 30 minutes

Serves 4. 206 calories per serving. Freeze ✗

Serves 4. 261 calories per serving. Freeze ✗

600 g (1 lb 5 oz) onions
low fat cooking spray
1 teaspoon caster sugar
1 tablespoon plain flour
1.5 litres (2¾ pints) hot vegetable stock
150 ml (¼ pint) dry white wine
8 x 2.5 cm (1 inch) thick slices of French stick
60 g (2 oz) half fat mature Cheddar cheese, grated
salt and freshly ground black pepper

200 g (7 oz) egg noodles
200 g (7 oz) sugar snap peas or mange tout, sliced lengthways
200 g (7 oz) carrots, sliced into thin matchsticks
250 g (9 oz) tofu, diced
a small bunch of fresh coriander, chopped
salt and freshly ground black pepper
For the soup
1.5 litres (2¾ pints) vegetable stock
1 garlic clove, peeled
1 stick of lemongrass, chopped roughly or 1 tablespoon dried lemongrass
1 small red chilli
1 star anise
1 cm (½ inch) fresh ginger, grated

● Slice the onions very finely – the quickest way to do this is in a food processor. Heat a large saucepan and spray with the low fat cooking spray. Add the onions, sprinkle with sugar and sauté for 20 minutes. Season.

● Stir frequently to get any caramelized onions off the bottom of the pan. Add the flour and cook, stirring, for a few minutes.

● Add the hot stock, more seasoning and wine and continue stirring with a wooden spoon to prevent the mixture from sticking to the bottom of the pan. Bring to the boil. Reduce the heat, cover and simmer with a lid for 15 minutes.

● Meanwhile, preheat the grill to High. Toast the bread slices on one side, then turn and place, toasted sides down, on a baking sheet and cover each slice with grated cheese. Grill for 2–3 minutes until the cheese is bubbling and golden. Pour the hot soup into a large, warmed tureen or four warmed soup bowls. Float the croûtons on top, then serve.

● Place all the soup ingredients in a saucepan and bring to the boil. Simmer for 10 minutes.

● Meanwhile, cook the noodles by placing them in a bowl and pouring boiling water over them and leaving them to stand for 10 minutes, stirring occasionally. Drain and place in the bottom of four serving bowls.

● Strain the soup, return to the saucepan and bring back to a simmer. Add the sugar snap peas or mange tout and the carrots. Simmer for 2 minutes, so that the vegetables are still crunchy. Season to taste.

● Pile the tofu on top of the noodles in the bowls and pour the soup over. Sprinkle with chopped coriander.

How to ...

sweat onions.
Slice the onions finely and place in a large saucepan. Spray with low fat cooking spray and add a pinch of sugar. Cook over a low heat for 20 minutes allowing the onions to caramelize, to bring out their flavour.

Butter bean and rosemary soup

10 POINTS values per recipe takes 10 minutes to prepare,
20 minutes to cook

Serves 4. 158 calories per serving. Freeze ❄

low fat cooking spray
2 garlic cloves, crushed
1 large onion, diced
1 large carrot, diced
4 rosemary sprigs, chopped finely
1.2 litres (2 pints) vegetable stock
3 x 300 g cans of butter beans, drained and rinsed
salt and freshly ground black pepper

● Spray a large saucepan with the low fat cooking spray and gently fry the garlic, onion and carrot for about 5 minutes, until beginning to soften. Add a little water if necessary to prevent the vegetables from sticking,

● Add the rosemary, stock and beans and bring to the boil. Cover and simmer for 15 minutes or until the carrots are cooked.

● Liquidise the soup and then return it to the saucepan to heat through. Season to taste, then serve.

 Minestrone primavera

A **simple** and **satisfying** springtime soup, filled with wonderful fresh vegetables and made **luxurious** by the soft cheese. Guaranteed to hit the spot everytime.

1 POINTS values per recipe takes 15 minutes to prepare,
20 minutes to cook

Serves 4. 139 calories per serving. Freeze ❄

low fat cooking spray
2 leeks, chopped finely
2 celery stalks, diced finely
400 g (14 oz) canned chopped tomatoes
450 g (1 lb) courgettes, diced finely
4 carrots, diced finely
200 g (7 oz) green beans, sliced finely
1 teaspoon dried Mediterranean herbs
1.2 litres (2 pints) vegetable stock
1 bunch of flat leafed parsley or basil, chopped
salt and freshly ground black pepper
4 teaspoons low fat soft cheese with garlic and herbs, to serve

● Spray a large saucepan with the low fat cooking spray. Sauté the leeks and celery, adding a little water if necessary to prevent them from sticking. After 5 minutes, add the chopped tomatoes, all the other vegetables and the dried herbs. Mix everything together and then pour over the stock. Bring to the boil and simmer for 10 minutes.

● Add some seasoning and the chopped parsley or basil. Serve each portion topped with a teaspoon of the soft cheese and a grinding of black pepper.

How to ●●●

make your own vegetable stock.

Reserve all the trimmings and peelings from vegetables and boil them in a pan with 1.2 litres (2 pints) water, a handful of peppercorns, 1/2 onion, a bay leaf and some herbs. Cook for 1 hour, then remove from the heat and strain. The stock will keep in the fridge for a few days or can be frozen.

Carrot and coriander soup

Enjoy the **classic combination** of carrots with coriander in this delicious soup.

Ⓨ *0 POINTS values per recipe* takes 15 minutes to prepare, 15 minutes to cook

Serves 4. 104 calories per serving. Freeze ❄

> low fat cooking spray
> 1 large onion, peeled and sliced thinly
> 1 kg (2 lb 4 oz) carrots, peeled and chopped roughly
> 1.2 litres (2 pints) vegetable stock
> a bunch of fresh coriander including roots if possible, washed
>   and chopped
> salt and freshly ground black pepper

● Spray a large non stick saucepan with the low fat cooking spray and stir fry the onion for 5 minutes, until softened, adding a little water if necessary to prevent it from sticking.

● Add the carrots, stock, seasoning and half of the coriander. Bring to the boil, then simmer for 15 minutes, until the carrots are tender. Add the rest of the coriander, reserving a little for garnishing.

● Liquidise the soup in batches and return to the pan. Warm through, check the seasoning and then serve garnished with the reserved coriander, and a grinding of black pepper.

 ## Smooth gazpacho

Here's a quick and easy version of this lovely **refreshing** soup. It's usually served chilled but can be gently warmed, if you prefer.

Ⓨ *0 POINTS values per recipe* takes 10 minutes + 30 minutes chilling

Serves 2. 96 calories per serving. Freeze ✗

> 450 g (1 lb) ripe tomatoes, chopped roughly
> ½ cucumber, peeled and chopped roughly
> 1 small red onion, chopped roughly
> 1 garlic clove, crushed
> 1 red pepper, de-seeded and chopped roughly
> 1 tablespoon wine vinegar
> a small bunch of parsley, basil or mint,
>   chopped roughly (with a little chopped
>   finely for garnishing)
> salt and freshly ground black pepper
> a few ice cubes, to serve

● Blend all the ingredients in a food processor, apart from the ice cubes and seasoning, then pour into a bowl. (If you prefer a smooth soup, strain it by pushing through a sieve.) Season.

● Chill for at least 30 minutes and then stir and serve with a few ice cubes in each soup bowl. Garnish each bowl with the finely chopped herbs.

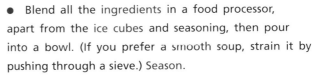

How to ...

add a special touch.

Place tiny sprigs of fresh herbs and/or herb flowers such as thyme or chives with the water in the ice tray. Freeze to make pretty ice cubes to serve with this soup.

Lush lentil soup

A lovely **wholesome** and totally **satisfying** soup.

23 POINTS values per recipe takes 10 minutes to prepare, 1 hour to cook

Serves 6. 288 calories per serving. Freeze ❄

> low fat cooking spray
> 1 large onion, peeled and chopped
> 4 garlic cloves, crushed
> 2 stalks celery, with leaves if possible, chopped
> 1 large carrot, peeled and chopped
> 500 g (1 lb 2 oz) red lentils
> 2 litres (3½ pints) vegetable stock
> 2 bay leaves
> 15 g (½ oz) porcini, soaked in 100 ml (3½ fl oz) boiling water
> for 10 minutes
> juice of ½ a lemon
> salt and freshly ground black pepper

● Heat a large non stick saucepan and spray with the low fat cooking spray. Stir fry the onion, garlic, celery and carrot for 5 minutes, until softened, adding a little water if necessary to stop them sticking.

● Add the lentils, stock and bay leaves and bring to the boil. Skim if necessary and simmer gently, covered, for 45 minutes, until the lentils are very soft. Meanwhile finely chop the porcini.

● Only after the lentils are cooked, season the soup and add the mushrooms with their strained soaking liquid. Simmer for a further 5 minutes then squeeze in the lemon and serve.

How to ...

enhance the mushroom flavour.

Soak the porcini and then strain them through a piece of muslin or very fine mesh strainer to remove any grit. Reserve the strained soaking liquid, finely chop the porcini, and incorporate them with the soaking liquid into your recipes to enhance the flavour of your dishes.

 Quick mussel soup

A quick, **warming** and **delicious** soup – great for the cold winter months.

12½ POINTS values per recipe takes 20 minutes to prepare, 20 minutes to cook

Serves 4. 263 calories per serving. Freeze ✗

> low fat cooking spray
> 1 large onion, chopped finely
> 1 celery stick, chopped finely
> 1 carrot, chopped finely
> 300 g (10½ oz) sweet potatoes or potatoes, diced into
> 1 cm (½ inch) cubes
> 1.2 litres (2 pints) vegetable stock
> 2 x 400 g cans of chopped tomatoes
> 450 g (1 lb) canned mussels
> 200g (7 oz) green beans, chopped
> a small bunch of soft thyme, chopped
> salt and freshly ground black pepper

● Heat a large non stick saucepan and spray with the low fat cooking spray. Stir fry the onion, celery, carrot and potatoes for a few minutes. Then add the stock and bring to the boil.

● Simmer for 10 minutes, then add the tomatoes. Simmer for a further 10 minutes. Finally, add the mussels, beans and thyme. Simmer gently for 2 minutes. Season to taste.

● Check that the potatoes are tender, then serve.

Courgette and mint soup

A **tasty** way to enjoy courgettes in this great summertime soup.

0 POINTS values per recipe takes 30 minutes

Serves 4. 61 calories per serving. Freeze ❄

low fat cooking spray
1 large onion, sliced finely
1 kg (2 lb 4 oz) courgettes, chopped roughly
1.2 litres (2 pints) vegetable stock
a bunch of fresh mint, chopped
salt and freshly ground black pepper

● Spray a large non stick saucepan with the low fat cooking spray and stir fry the onion for 5 minutes, until softened, adding a little water if necessary to prevent it from sticking.

● Add the courgettes, stock, seasoning and half the mint. Bring to the boil and then simmer for 10 minutes, until the courgettes are tender. Add most of the remaining mint, reserving a little for garnishing.

● Liquidise the soup in batches, in a blender, and then return to the pan. Warm through, check the seasoning and then serve garnished with the reserved mint and a grinding of black pepper.

 ## Roasted pumpkin soup

A **fantastic** soup for autumn, with a **beautiful** orange colour. Roasting creates a more intense flavour and the Chinese five spice powder gives it added warmth.

0 POINTS values per recipe takes 20 minutes to prepare, 40 minutes to cook

Serves 4. 46 calories per serving. Freeze ❄

low fat cooking spray
6 shallots, unpeeled and cut in half
2 garlic cloves, unpeeled and crushed
750 g (1 lb 10 oz) pumpkin, peeled, de-seeded and chopped roughly
2 teaspoons Chinese five spice powder
1.2 litres (2 pints) vegetable stock
salt and freshly ground black pepper
a small bunch of fresh chives, chopped, to garnish

● Preheat the oven to Gas Mark 7/220°C/fan oven 200°C and spray a large roasting tray with the low fat cooking spray. Add the shallots, garlic and pumpkin. Toss with the seasoning and Chinese five spice powder.

● Roast for 30 minutes, stirring occasionally, until softened and slightly charred. When cool enough to handle, peel the skins from the shallots and garlic, then transfer everything to a large saucepan and add the stock. Bring to the boil and simmer for 10 minutes.

● Liquidise the soup in batches and return to the pan to warm through. Check the seasoning and serve with a scattering of chives.

How to ...

make your POINTS values go further.

Both of these soups have zero POINTS values and can be eaten freely on both food plans. To ensure that you always have a tasty snack to fill you up, make up large batches of these soups and freeze them for a quick filler.

Snack attack

Snack attacks happen to us all. The trick is to enjoy snacking without it spiralling out of control. Think carefully about the snacks you eat – and prepare for when these moments strike – so that you can enjoy snacks without the guilt, knowing that you are keeping your weight loss in check. In order to be rewarding, snacks don't have to be laden with fat and calories – in fact, if you make wise ingredient choices you can create satisfying nibbles that will allow you to really make the most of those 'snacking' occasions. This chapter shows you how to create tempting and tasty munchies that are much more satisfying then convenience snacks – and you can really enjoy them without worrying about your weight loss progress.

Bombay popcorn (page 18)

[satisfying]

Bombay popcorn

A fantastic and fun low *POINTS* value snack to enjoy in front of the telly.

5 *POINTS values per recipe* takes 15 minutes

Serves 4. 37 calories per serving. Freeze ✗

1 teaspoon vegetable oil

75 g (2³/₄ oz) corn kernels

2 tablespoons soy sauce

1 teaspoon curry powder, e.g. garam masala

salt and freshly ground black pepper

● Heat the oil in a large saucepan with a lid until nearly smoking. Add the corn and put the lid on the pan. Shake vigorously from time to time over a medium high heat until you hear the corn starting to pop.

● Shake the pan until you no longer hear popping, then remove from the heat and tip into a large bowl.

● Shake over the soy sauce, curry powder and seasoning, then replace the lid and shake again until the popcorn is evenly coated. Eat warm or cold.

How to ●●●

save time.

Place the oil in a microwavable bowl and heat for one minute. Add the corn kernels and cover with a plate. Microwave for 2–3 minutes until the pops are about 5 seconds apart. Carefully remove the plate, add the soy sauce, curry powder and seasoning and shake to coat.

 Curried cauliflower fritters

These delicious little fritters are great as a low *POINTS* value starter, or to serve at a buffet.

4¹/₂ *POINTS values per recipe* takes 30 minutes + 30 minutes standing (optional)

Serves 4. 90 calories per serving. Freeze ✗

200 g (7 oz) cauliflower, sliced and broken into small florets

3 tablespoons plain flour

1 teaspoon curry powder, e.g. garam masala

1 egg, separated

3 tablespoons skimmed milk

low fat cooking spray

salt and freshly ground black pepper

For the dip

5 cm (2 inches) fresh root ginger, grated finely

3 tablespoons soy sauce

3 tablespoons rice vinegar

● Blanch the cauliflower florets in boiling, salted water for a few minutes, until just tender.

● Meanwhile place the flour in a bowl with the curry powder and season. Add the egg yolk to the flour.

● Stir in the yolk and the milk, mixing thoroughly, then add the cauliflower, 3 tablespoons of the cauliflower cooking liquid and fold gently together. Set aside for about 30 minutes, if you have time.

● Meanwhile, make the dip by mixing all the dip ingredients together in a small bowl.

● Beat the egg white until stiff and gently fold into the batter mix with a large metal spoon. Heat a large frying pan and spray with the low fat cooking spray, then drop in tablespoonfuls of the batter.

● Cook five or six fritters at the same time, for 3–4 minutes. Flip over with a palette knife and cook the other side for 3–4 minutes, until golden brown. Keep warm on a plate while you cook the others, then serve with the dip.

Falafels with Moroccan orange salad

 Warm spicy sausage and spinach salad

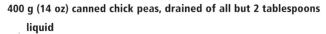

24¹/2 POINTS values per recipe takes 30 minutes to prepare, 40–45 minutes to bake + soaking

Serves 6. 294 calories per serving. Freeze after step 2 ❄

- 400 g (14 oz) canned chick peas, drained of all but 2 tablespoons liquid
- 250 g (9 oz) dried chick peas, soaked for at least 2 hours, preferably overnight
- 1 small garlic clove
- 1 tablespoon tahini paste
- 4 spring onions, chopped finely
- a small bunch of fresh coriander, chopped
- 1 teaspoon ground coriander
- 1 teaspoon ground cumin
- ¹/4 teaspoon dried chilli flakes or more to taste
- juice of 1 lemon
- low fat cooking spray
- salt and freshly ground black pepper

For the salad

- 4 carrots, grated coarsely
- 200 g (7 oz) cabbage, shredded finely
- 2 oranges, peeled and cut into segments, reserving any juice
- 1 orange, juiced
- 25 g (1 oz) flaked almonds, toasted

● Preheat the oven to Gas Mark 4/180°C/fan oven 160°C. Place the soaked chick peas in a food processor. Process to a paste-like consistency, stopping to scrape the sides and stir the mixture.
● Add the other ingredients, apart from the salad and low fat cooking spray, including the 2 tablespoons of liquid from the canned chick peas. Process, stopping and stirring occasionally, until the mixture holds together when you roll it into walnut size balls in your hands. (The mixture will make about 30 balls.)
● Place on a non stick baking tray sprayed with the low fat cooking spray. Bake for 40–45 minutes until golden.
● Meanwhile, make the salad by gently tossing all the ingredients together with seasoning.

7 POINTS values per recipe takes 25–30 minutes

Serves 2. 292 calories per serving. Freeze ✗

- 4 thick low fat sausages
- 150 g (5¹/2 oz) cherry tomatoes
- 225 g (8 oz) baby spinach, washed
- salt and freshly ground black pepper

For the dressing

- 1 tablespoon balsamic vinegar
- 1 small red chilli, de-seeded and chopped finely or ¹/4 teaspoon dried chilli flakes
- 1 small garlic clove, crushed
- 2 teaspoons olive oil

● Preheat the oven to Gas Mark 7/220°C/fan oven 200°C. Place the sausages and tomatoes in a roasting tin. Season and bake for 15–20 minutes, shaking the tin occasionally, until the sausages are browned and the tomatoes softened. Once the sausages are cooked, slice them diagonally into bite sized pieces.
● Mix together the dressing ingredients in a medium size bowl and add the spinach. Season, then toss together. Divide between two serving bowls. Spoon the hot tomatoes and sausage slices on top and serve.

Chicken Waldorf salad

9¹/₂ POINTS values per recipe takes 10 minutes

Serves 2. 336 calories per serving. Freeze ✗

1 large red dessert apple, cored and sliced thinly

100 g (3¹/₂ oz) smoked or roast chicken, skinned and cubed

4 celery sticks, sliced thinly

¹/₂ small red cabbage, shredded thinly

30 g (1¹/₄ oz) walnut pieces

150 g (5¹/₂ oz) mixed salad leaves

a small bunch of chives, sliced finely

For the dressing

1 teaspoon Dijon mustard

juice of 1 orange (about 3 tablespoons)

2 tablespoons low fat mayonnaise

● Put all the salad ingredients, apart from the mixed leaves and chives, in a large bowl.

● Shake all the dressing ingredients together in an empty jam jar and then pour over the salad. Toss together. Arrange the mixed leaves on serving plates or in bowls, then pile the salad on top.

● Scatter with the chives, and serve.

 Chicken satay

4¹/₂ POINTS values per recipe takes 25 minutes + 30 minutes soaking + 15 minutes marinating

Serves 1. 260 calories per serving. Freeze ❄

1 medium (165 g/5³/₄ oz) skinless, boneless chicken breast, sliced into 4 long strips

For the marinade

1 garlic clove, crushed

2.5 cm (1 inch) piece of fresh root ginger, peeled and grated finely

1 tablespoon soy sauce

1 teaspoon runny honey

grated zest and juice of 1 lime

For the peanut sauce

1 teaspoon crunchy peanut butter

1 tablespoon reduced fat coconut milk

salt and freshly ground black pepper

● Soak four long wooden skewers in water for about 30 minutes, to stop them from burning under the grill.

● Meanwhile, mix together the marinade ingredients in a bowl and add the chicken strips. Toss together, coating the chicken, then leave in the fridge for at least 15 minutes or overnight.

● Preheat the grill to high, drain the marinade into a small saucepan and thread one strip of chicken on to each skewer. Grill for 3 minutes on each side, until golden brown and cooked through, brushing every now and then with the marinade.

● Bring the remaining marinade to the boil for a minute or so and then add the peanut sauce ingredients and a tablespoon of water if the sauce is too thick. Stir together until well blended. Serve the satay skewers with the peanut sauce for dipping.

How to ●●●

make the most of the flavour.

Use marinades to add flavour to meat and fish. Place the meat into the marinade ingredients and leave for as long as possible, preferably overnight, to draw out the flavour.

Vegetable samosas

These samosas are very low in *POINTS* values and are ideal for buffets and snacks.

Ⓨ *10 POINTS values per recipe* takes 1 hour to prepare, 15 minutes to cook

Makes 24. 37 calories per serving. Freeze ✗

2 carrots, peeled and diced

low fat cooking spray

2 shallots or 1 small onion, chopped finely

1 garlic clove, chopped finely

150 g (5½ oz) fresh or frozen spinach

100 g (3½ oz) potatoes, peeled and diced

1 tablespoon Indian Balti or Tandoori curry paste

100 g (3½ oz) frozen peas

juice of ½ a lime

8 sheets of 28 x 43 cm (11 x 17 inches) filo pastry

salt and freshly ground black pepper

For the raita

4 tablespoons low fat plain yogurt

½ small garlic clove, crushed

a small bunch of mint, chopped finely plus extra, to garnish

● Boil the carrots until tender, then drain and set aside. Meanwhile, heat a non stick frying pan and spray with the low fat cooking spray. Fry the shallots or onion and garlic until golden, adding a little water if necessary to prevent them from sticking.

● Add the carrot, spinach, potatoes, curry paste, peas, lime juice and seasoning to the frying pan. Stir together and cook for 5 minutes.

● Preheat the oven to Gas Mark 7/220°C/fan oven 200°C.

● Lay one sheet of filo pastry on a clean, dry work surface and cut lengthways into three equal strips. Spray with the low fat cooking spray and place about 2 teaspoons of the vegetable mixture in the middle of the left hand end of the strip, about 1 cm (½ inch) from the end.

● Then pick up the bottom left hand corner of the pastry strip and fold over the vegetable mixture until what was the bottom edge lies along the top edge and you have a triangular shaped parcel with two open seams.

● Take hold of the top left hand corner and flip the whole parcel over, so that what was the top left corner becomes the top right corner. Now take the new top left corner and flip the parcel again by taking the corner down to lie along the bottom edge.

● All the time you are wrapping along the length of the filo pastry strip keeping the parcel in a triangular shape. Continue until all the pastry is used up and then spray the samosa with the low fat cooking spray. Lay it on a sprayed baking sheet. Repeat with the remaining filo pastry strips.

● Bake for 15 minutes, until the pastry is golden and crisp. Leave to cool slightly before eating. Meanwhile, make the raita by stirring together all the ingredients. Add a little seasoning. Spoon into a bowl to serve and garnish with mint sprigs.

How to ●●●

handle filo pastry.

If using frozen pastry, allow it to thaw in the pack and then take out the sheets and stack them on a cloth. While you work, cover the sheets with a slightly damp cloth and use the sheets one at a time, making sure you spray them well with the cooking spray. This will help to keep the filo moist as it dries out very quickly when exposed to the air.

Baby herb and cheese scones

Ⓨ *20¹/₂ POINTS values per recipe* takes 15 minutes to prepare, 15 minutes to bake

Makes 26. 47 calories per serving. Freeze ✗

225 g (8 oz) self raising flour, plus 1 tablespoon for dusting
¹/₄ teaspoon salt
40 g (1¹/₂ oz) polyunsaturated margarine, chilled
1 teaspoon dried herbs, e.g. oregano, marjoram or mixed herbs
50 g (1³/₄ oz) half fat mature Cheddar cheese, grated
¹/₂ teaspoon dried mustard
150 ml (¹/₄ pint) skimmed milk

● Preheat the oven to Gas Mark 7/220°C/fan oven 200°C. Line a baking tray with non stick baking paper.
● Sieve the flour into a large bowl. Mix in the salt. Cut the margarine into small pieces and add to the flour. Rub with your fingertips until the mixture resembles breadcrumbs. Stir in the herbs, cheese and mustard.
● Make a well in the centre, gradually stir in all but 2 tablespoons of the milk. Turn out on to a floured surface. Knead quickly and lightly.
● Press out the smooth dough gently with the palms of your hands to about 1 cm (¹/₂ inch) thick. Cut into rounds about 3 cm (1¹/₄ inches) in diameter. Place on the prepared baking sheet. Press together the trimmings and repeat the rolling and cutting process until the dough is used up.
● Brush the scones with the reserved milk and bake for 12–15 minutes, until risen and golden. Cool on a rack.

How to ●●●

knead dough.

Kneading should be done on a smooth surface. Turn out the dough and then fold it towards you. Quickly push down with the heel of your hand. Turn the dough and stretch it out. Repeat until the dough is firm and smooth. This will give the dough elasticity, allowing it to rise more easily.

 Tomato bread

This recipe contains no yeast so there's no waiting! It makes a **delicious** savoury bread that's **ideal** with soup or stews.

Ⓨ *17 POINTS values per recipe* takes 25 minutes to prepare, 15 minutes to bake

Serves 6. 189 calories per serving. Freeze ✗

225 g (8 oz) plain flour, plus extra for dusting
a pinch of salt
3 teaspoons baking powder
25 g (1 oz) sun dried tomatoes, soaked for 10 minutes in boiling water, then drained and chopped
4 spring onions, chopped finely
200 ml (7 fl oz) skimmed milk
2 tablespoons olive oil
salt and freshly ground black pepper

● Preheat the oven to Gas Mark 7/220°C/fan oven 200°C. Sift the flour, salt and baking powder into a large bowl. Grind in a little black pepper and stir in the chopped sun dried tomatoes and spring onions.
● Mix 150 ml (¹/₄ pint) of the milk and the oil together and add to the flour mixture. Gently combine to make a soft and manageable dough, adding the extra milk if necessary.
● On a lightly floured surface, roll out the dough to about 2.5 cm (1 inch) thick. Form into a round about 15 cm (6 inches) in diameter. Score into six triangles with a knife, taking care not to cut all the way through the dough.
● Place on a baking tray, lined with non stick baking paper and bake for 12–15 minutes, until the bread is risen and golden.

Roasted vegetable salad ✓

🅨 *½ POINTS values per recipe* takes 20 minutes to prepare, 30 minutes to roast

Serves 4. 190 calories per serving. Freeze ✗

1 butternut squash, peeled and cut into small chunks

4 carrots, peeled and cut into 4 short lengths on the diagonal

4 courgettes, cut into 4 short lengths on the diagonal

4 garlic cloves, unpeeled

2 small red onions, peeled and cut into wedges

low fat cooking spray

3 tablespoons balsamic vinegar

salt and freshly ground black pepper

For the salad

2 Little Gem lettuces, shredded

100 g (3½ oz) cherry tomatoes, halved

100 g (3½ oz) green beans or asparagus

juice of 1 small lemon

1 teaspoon wholegrain mustard

2 tablespoons very low fat plain fromage frais

● Preheat the oven to Gas Mark 7/220°C/fan oven 200°C and place all the vegetables, except the salad ingredients, in a roasting tray. Season, spray with the low fat cooking spray and sprinkle over the balsamic vinegar. Roast for 30 minutes, tossing occasionally until golden and softened.

● Meanwhile, prepare the salad. Place the lettuce on four serving plates or in a large serving bowl and top with the tomatoes and beans or asparagus. In a jam jar, shake together the lemon juice with the mustard, fromage frais and 2 tablespoons of water to make the dressing.

● Spoon the roasted vegetables on to the salad and pour over the dressing. Toss together and serve immediately.

How to ...

roast vegetables.

Select your vegetables according to your tastes or the season. Chop all of the vegetables into evenly sized pieces so that they all require the same amound of cooking time. Spray a baking tray with the low fat cooking spray, and place the vegetables, evenly distributed, onto the tray. Spray again with the cooking spray, sprinkle over a little balsamic vinegar, season and then cook in the oven until golden and soft.

2½ POINTS VALUE ## Watercress, prawn & mango salad

An unusual combination of ingredients that is sure to tantalise your taste buds.

5 POINTS values per recipe takes 20 minutes

Serves 2. 102 calories per serving. Freeze ✗

- 1 large ripe mango, stoned and skinned
- 85 g bag of watercress or baby spinach or rocket or mixed leaves, shredded
- 100 g (3½ oz) cooked, peeled prawns
- 1 small red chilli, de-seeded and chopped finely or 2 pinches of dried chilli flakes
- 2 cherry tomatoes, sliced into thin wedges

For the dressing
- juice of ½ a lemon
- 1 teaspoon wholegrain mustard
- 2 tablespoon very low fat plain fromage frais
- 1 teaspoon tomato purée
- sea salt and freshly ground black pepper

● Slice the mango in half. Slice each half four or five times, leave about 1 cm (½ inch) at the end so that the fruit can be fanned out. Divide the watercress between two serving plates or bowls.

● Place one mango fan over the top of each pile and divide the prawns between the two plates or bowls.

● Mix all the dressing ingredients together in a bowl and pour the mixture over the prawns, then sprinkle over the chopped chilli and decorate with the tomato wedges.

 **1½ POINTS VALUE** ## Cheesy garlic mushrooms

Keep this easy starter in mind for a **special** dinner – it's quick but **impressive**.

5 POINTS values per recipe takes 10 minutes to prepare,

20 minutes to cook

Serves 4. 93 calories per serving. Freeze ✗

- 10 large cup shaped field mushrooms, preferably portabello
- 200 g (7 oz) low fat soft cheese with garlic or onion and chives
- 4 cherry tomatoes, chopped
- 2 tablespoons soy sauce
- a small bunch of parsley, chopped finely
- salt and freshly ground black pepper

● Preheat the oven to Gas mark 4/180°C/fan oven 160°C and remove the stalks from eight of the mushrooms. Chop the stalks and the two whole mushrooms finely and place in a bowl with the cheese, tomatoes, soy sauce and seasoning and most of the parsley (reserving a little for the garnish).

● Beat the mixture together with a wooden spoon. Place the destalked mushrooms cup side up in a baking dish.

● Pile the cheese mixture into each mushroom and bake for 20 minutes, then serve scattered with the rest of the parsley.

How to ●●●

clean mushrooms.

Mushrooms have a distinct flavour. In order to retain the full flavour of the mushrooms you should not wash them, but rather gently wipe them clean with a damp cloth and then dry them with a paper towel.

Middle Eastern aubergine dip

This is a deliciously **different** sauce from the Middle East, known as Baba Ganoush, with a slightly **smoky** flavour that can be used on pasta or vegetables or as a dip.

(Y) *(if you use soya yogurt) 1½ POINTS values per recipe* takes 10 minutes to prepare, 1¼ hours to cook

Serves 4. 61 calories per serving. Freeze ✗

1 kg (2 lb 4 oz) aubergines

½ small onion, chopped coarsely

2 garlic cloves

juice of 1 lemon

a small bunch of flat leafed parsley, chopped

150 g (5½ oz) low fat plain yogurt

salt and freshly ground black pepper

a pinch of cayenne pepper or paprika, to serve

- Preheat the oven to Gas Mark 7/220°C/fan oven 200°C. Prick the aubergines with a fork and lay them on a baking tray. Sprinkle with salt, then roast for 35–45 minutes or until charred and soft. Leave to cool.
- Slit the cooled aubergines open. Spoon the flesh out of them and put into a food processor with the onion, garlic, lemon juice, parsley and yogurt to blend.
- Taste and adjust the seasoning and then serve sprinkled with a pinch of cayenne pepper or paprika.

How to ●●●

choose an aubergine.

Aubergines can vary in colour, so this is not necessarily a good indicator. Look for firm, heavy aubergines that have no brown patches and a cleft at the wider end. Before using aubergines, sprinkle salt on the flesh, leave for 30 minutes and then rinse.

 ## Houmous with roasted vegetables

A **tasty** new way to make and serve houmous.

(Y) *8½ POINTS values per recipe* takes 20 minutes to prepare, 35 minutes to cook

Serves 2. 488 calories per serving. Freeze ✗

4 large carrots, cut in half crossways and then into wedges

2 courgettes, cut in half crossways and then into wedges

250 g (9 oz) sweet potatoes, peeled and cut into wedges

½ cauliflower, divided into large florets

2 tablespoons balsamic vinegar

low fat cooking spray

1 large red pepper, halved and de-seeded

300 g (10½ oz) canned chick peas

1 garlic clove, crushed

juice of ½ lemon

salt and freshly ground black pepper

- Preheat the oven to Gas Mark 8/230°C/fan oven 210°C. Place the first four vegetables in a large roasting tray and sprinkle with the balsamic vinegar and seasoning. Spray with the low fat cooking spray.
- Lay the pepper halves on top of the other vegetables, skin side up. Roast for 35 minutes, turning the vegetables occasionally with a fish slice to prevent them from sticking to the bottom.
- Remove the pepper halves after 15–20 minutes, when the skin has blistered and charred. Wrap in a plastic bag and set aside until cool enough to handle. Then peel away the skin and chop roughly. Leave the other vegetables to continue roasting.
- Drain the chick peas, reserving the liquid and put into a food processor with the peeled and roughly chopped grilled pepper, garlic, lemon juice and seasoning. Add enough of the chick pea liquid to allow you to process the houmous to a smooth purée.
- Check the seasoning and spoon the houmous into a serving bowl. Place the bowl on a large platter and serve with the roasted vegetables around it for dipping.

Houmous with roasted vegetables

③ Tropical fruit kebabs

POINTS VALUE

Ⓨ **11 POINTS values per recipe** takes 20 minutes to prepare

Serves 4. 143 calories per serving. Freeze ✗

4 figs, halved
½ pineapple, cut into segments
8 large strawberries
2 bananas, cut into 2.5 cm (1 inch) lengths
2 peaches, quartered
juice and grated zest of 2 oranges
200 g (7 oz) low fat yogurt in any flavour, to serve

● Soak eight wooden kebab sticks in water for at least 10 minutes to prevent them from burning.
● Thread five or six pieces of fruit on to each of eight wooden kebab sticks and place the kebabs in a large, shallow dish.
● Mix the juice and grated zest together and pour over the kebabs. Leave to marinate for 10 minutes before placing under a grill or on a barbecue. Cook until the fruit starts to soften and turn golden at the edges. Serve with a bowl of low fat yogurt for dipping.

②½ Banana cake

POINTS VALUE

26 POINTS values per recipe takes 25 minutes to prepare, 30 minutes to bake + cooling

Serves 10. 168 calories per serving. Freeze ❄ cake for up to 1 month. The filling cannot be frozen.

150 g (5½ oz) low fat soft cheese
4 tablespoons artificial sweetener
3 medium eggs, separated
2 soft bananas, peeled and mashed with a fork
200 g (7 oz) polenta, cooked according to packet instructions
½ teaspoon baking powder
low fat cooking spray
For the filling
150 g (5½ oz) low fat soft cheese
1½ teaspoons artificial sweetener
grated zest of 1 orange
1 banana
juice of ½ lemon

● Preheat the oven to Gas Mark 4/180°C/fan oven 160°C.
● Cream together the low fat soft cheese and the sweetener and then whisk in the egg yolks and mashed banana.
● Fold in the polenta and baking powder. Whisk the egg whites in a separate bowl, until stiff. Fold them into the polenta mixture.
● Spray two 18 cm (7 inch) tins with low fat cooking spray and line the base with greaseproof paper. Divide the mixture between two tins and bake for 30 minutes or until firm to the touch.
● Allow the cakes to rest for 5 minutes and then remove from the tins. Leave to cool on a cooling rack.
● For the filling, cream together the low fat soft cheese, sweetener and orange zest and spread over one of the cakes.
● Slice the banana and toss in the lemon juice before placing on top of the creamy filling. Place the other cake on top and serve.

Fast and fabulous

When there are so many ready meals out there that can be rustled up in minutes, it can sometimes be difficult to see the point in cooking from scratch – particularly when you are tired after a hard day at work or in a rush to get on. However, ready meals are often full of artificial ingredients, saturated fat and calories and the feeling of satisfaction tends to be short-lived. You are much more likely to feel full for longer if you cook from home – and you can be confident that you are eating fresh, wholesome foods that will help you to lose weight and keep it off. Cooking doesn't have to be stressful – there are so many delicious meals that can be created in minutes. Just have a look through this chapter for some inspiration.

Cherry tomato pizza (page 38)

Chicken laksa

Laksas are Malaysian soupy noodle curries made with a dizzying array of ingredients.

15½ POINTS values per recipe takes 30 minutes

Serves 4. 260 calories per serving. Freeze ✗

low fat cooking spray

2 garlic cloves, crushed

2 teaspoons Thai red or green curry paste

400 g (14 oz) skinless, boneless chicken breast fillets, cut into small pieces

3 tablespoons soy sauce

300 ml (½ pint) chicken stock

100 g (3½ oz) fine egg or rice noodles, broken up

1 teaspoon sugar

1 lemongrass stalk, chopped into 4 pieces and crushed slightly

5 kaffir lime leaves, rolled up and sliced finely crossways

2 tablespoons low fat coconut milk

20 g (¾ oz) roasted peanuts, chopped, to garnish

a small bunch of fresh coriander, chopped, to garnish

● Heat a wok or large frying pan, spray with low fat cooking spray and fry the garlic until golden brown, adding a little water, if necessary, to prevent it from sticking. Add the curry paste and stir fry for 30 seconds.

● Add the chicken pieces and stir briefly until thoroughly coated with the paste. Add the soy sauce, stock, noodles and sugar and cook for a further 2 minutes.

● Add the lemongrass and lime leaves. Lower the heat and simmer for 10 minutes.

● Remove the lemongrass sticks and stir in the coconut milk. Spoon into dishes to serve, garnished with the peanuts and coriander.

 Thai chicken curry

A delicious Thai curry, **highly flavoured** and hot. Serve with 4 tablespoons of cooked, plain rice and steamed green beans, broccoli or pak choi, sprinkled with soy sauce for an extra *POINTS* value of 3.

14 POINTS values per recipe takes 20 minutes

Serves 4. 230 calories per serving. Freeze ✗

low fat cooking spray

2 garlic cloves, crushed

2 onions, chopped

2.5 cm (1 inch) piece of fresh root ginger, peeled and chopped finely

4 x 165 g (5¾ oz) skinless, boneless chicken breasts, cut in bite size pieces

1–2 teaspoons Thai green or red curry paste

3 tablespoons soy sauce

grated zest and juice of 1 lime

125 ml (4 fl oz) chicken stock

½ teaspoon sugar

100 g (3½ oz) watercress

a small bunch of fresh coriander, chopped roughly

1 tablespoon peanuts, toasted and chopped, to garnish

● Heat a non stick wok or large frying pan on a high heat, spray with the low fat cooking spray and fry the garlic, onions and ginger quickly, until golden brown, adding a little water, if necessary, to prevent them from sticking.

● Add the chicken pieces and brown them all over. Then add the curry paste and stir until the chicken is coated, Add the soy sauce, lime zest and juice, stock and sugar and cook for a further 2 minutes.

● Add the watercress and coriander, reserving a little coriander to garnish, and cook for a final 2 minutes. If the mixture begins to dry out, add a little more water although the curry is meant to be quite dry.

● Serve garnished with the peanuts and reserved coriander.

3 POINTS VALUE

Cod and chorizo kebabs

12 POINTS values per recipe takes 30 minutes

Serves 4. 179 calories per serving. Freeze ✗

- **85 g pack of thinly sliced chorizo or spicy salami, each slice halved**
- **500 g (1 lb 2 oz) cod fillets, skinned and cut in 5 cm (2 inch) cubes**
- **4 courgettes, cut into 6 thick diagonal slices**
- **2 tablespoons soy sauce**

● Thread one corner of a half piece of chorizo on to a skewer, then add a cube of cod then a slice of courgette and then another half piece of chorizo. Repeat until you have three or so cubes of cod, halves of sausage and courgette slices on each skewer.

● Place the soy sauce on a plate and then put the skewers on the plate and turn until they are covered in the sauce. Also brush sauce on to the fish with a pastry brush.

● Place the skewers on a piece of foil on the grill pan or put straight on to the hot barbecue or griddle. Grill for 3–4 minutes, turn and brush again. Grill for a further 3–4 minutes until the fish is cooked through and the chorizo golden.

 3 POINTS VALUE

Prawn stir fry

A very quick recipe that is satisfying and full of robust flavours.

12 POINTS values per recipe takes 15 minutes

Serves 4. 208 calories per serving. Freeze ✗

- **125 g (4¹/₂ oz) rice noodles**
- **boiling water, to soak**
- **low fat cooking spray**
- **1 large garlic clove, crushed**
- **200 g (7 oz) large prawns, peeled and de-veined**
- **2 tablespoons soy sauce**
- **1 teaspoon caster sugar**
- **juice of 1 lime**
- **100 g (3¹/₂ oz) beansprouts**
- **75 g (2³/₄ oz) radishes, chopped**
- **2 carrots, peeled and sliced into matchsticks**
- **20 g (³/₄ oz) peanuts, chopped**
- To garnish
- **2 shallots, chopped finely**
- **a small bunch of fresh coriander, chopped**
- **1 teaspoon dried chilli flakes**

● Soak the noodles for 5 minutes in boiling water or as instructed on the packet.

● Meanwhile, heat a wok or large non stick frying pan, spray with the low fat cooking spray and add the garlic, stir frying for a couple of minutes until golden brown and adding a little water, if necessary, to prevent it from sticking.

● Add the prawns and stir fry for a further 2 minutes. Stir in the soy sauce, sugar and lime juice.

● Drain the noodles and snip into smaller lengths with scissors. Toss together with the beansprouts, radishes, carrots and peanuts in the pan. Stir fry for a final 2 minutes and then serve immediately, garnished with the shallots, coriander and chilli flakes.

Cherry tomato pizza

Ⓨ *8 POINTS values per recipe* takes 30 minutes

Serves 1. 431 calories per serving. Freeze ✗

60 g (2 oz) self raising flour

a pinch of salt

15 g (½ oz) polyunsaturated margarine

a pinch of dried Mediterranean herbs, e.g. oregano, marjoram
  or basil

4 tablespoons skimmed milk

low fat cooking spray

about 10 cherry tomatoes, halved

40 g (1½ oz) half fat Cheddar cheese, grated

salt and freshly ground black pepper

fresh basil leaves, to garnish

● Preheat the oven to Gas Mark 7/220°C/fan oven 200°C. Place a baking tray in the oven to heat up.
● Sieve the flour into a bowl and mix in the salt. Add the margarine in pieces and rub together with your fingertips until the margarine is evenly distributed. Stir in the herbs.
● Make a well in the centre, pour in the milk and gradually stir into the mixture. Pull together with your fingers to form a rough dough ball. Add a little more milk if necessary but take care not to make the dough too wet; it just needs to stick together.
● Spray the heated baking sheet with the low fat cooking spray and then place the dough on the baking sheet. Push with your fingers and roll with a rolling pin to a circle about 5 mm (¼ inch) thick. Pile on the tomatoes and sprinkle over the cheese.
● Season and then bake for 10–12 minutes, until golden around the edges. Serve hot, scattered with fresh basil leaves.

How to ●●●

save time.

You can buy thin crust 9 inch pizza bases from the supermarket instead of making your own. Simply pile on the topping above and cook according to the packet instructions. The POINTS values per serving remain the same.

 Oriental style turkey leftovers

This is a tasty and unusual way to use up some of the leftover Christmas turkey and vegetables.

4½ POINTS values per recipe takes 20 minutes

Serves 2. 220 calories per serving. Freeze ✗

200 g (7 oz) cooked turkey meat

low fat cooking spray

2.5 cm (1 inch) piece of fresh root ginger, peeled and sliced
  into matchsticks

2 garlic cloves, sliced finely

about 400 g (14 oz) leftover cooked zero *POINTS* value vegetables,
  e.g. Brussels sprouts, shredded; carrots, sliced finely; cabbage,
  shredded

1–2 tablespoons soy sauce

1 tablespoon runny honey

2 tablespoons rice vinegar or white wine vinegar

salt and freshly ground black pepper

a small bunch of fresh coriander, parsley or mint, chopped,
  to garnish

● Shred the cooked turkey meat as finely as possible. Heat a large non stick frying pan and spray with the low fat cooking spray. Stir fry the ginger and garlic for 2 minutes or until golden.
● Add the vegetables, turkey, soy sauce, honey, vinegar and seasoning and stir fry together until thoroughly heated through. Scatter with the herbs and serve at once.

5 POINTS VALUE | Quick pesto pasta

The ultimate in quick, satisfying dinners, this is a bright and beautiful plate of crisp summer vegetables with pesto and pasta.

if you use vegan pesto sauce. 5 POINTS values per recipe takes 25 minutes

Serves 1. 412 calories per serving. Freeze ✗

low fat cooking spray
60 g (2 oz) dried pasta shapes, cooked according to pack instructions
100 g (3¹/2 oz) snow peas
50 g (1³/4 oz) frozen petits pois
100 g (3¹/2 oz) broccoli
100 g (3¹/2 oz) cherry tomatoes, halved
1 tablespoon pesto sauce
salt and freshly ground black pepper

● Heat a wok or large frying pan, spray with the low fat cooking spray and then steam fry the pasta and vegetables with 3 tablespoons of water for 2–3 minutes.

● Add the pesto sauce and seasoning, heat through and then serve.

How to ●●●

steam-fry.

Turn the heat up to high and allow the pan to get hot. Spray with low fat cooking spray and then add a little water or stock. The water will turn to steam almost immediately and this will cook the food. Vary the vegetables with your favourite zero varieties, making sure that you cut any larger vegetables into small, evenly sized pieces so that they cook quickly and at the same rate.

4 POINTS VALUE | Piedmont peppers

8 POINTS values per recipe takes 30 minutes

Serves 2. 232 calories per serving. Freeze ✗

2 large red peppers, halved and de-seeded
16 cherry tomatoes, halved
100 g (3¹/2 oz) feta cheese, cubed
2 tablespoons balsamic vinegar
a small bunch of fresh basil, leaves only
salt and freshly ground black pepper

● Preheat the oven to Gas Mark 4/180°C/fan oven 160°C and place the peppers, skin side down, on a baking tray. In a bowl, toss the tomatoes with the other ingredients and fill the pepper shells with this mixture.

● Bake for 20 minutes, until softened and slightly charred, then serve.

Beef stir fry

A delicately flavoured stir fry that is so quick and easy to prepare. Serve with 4 tablespoons of plain boiled rice for an extra **POINTS** value of 3 per serving.

4¹/2 POINTS values per recipe takes 20 minutes

Serves 2. 165 calories per serving. Freeze ✗

low fat cooking spray
2 garlic cloves, chopped finely
150 g (5¹/2 oz) lean beef steak, cut into thin strips
1 red pepper, de-seeded and sliced finely
1 small red or green chilli, de-seeded and chopped finely
2 heads of pak choi or spring greens, shredded
2 tablespoons soy sauce
2 tablespoons oyster or black bean sauce
juice of 1 lime

● Heat a wok or frying pan, spray with the low fat cooking spray and fry the garlic until golden brown. Add the beef strips and stir fry until just cooked through, about 4 minutes.
● Add all the remaining ingredients in turn and continue to stir fry for approximately 5 minutes. Serve immediately.

How to ●●●

slice meats evenly.

To cut meats into thin, even slices without damaging the meat, simply place the whole cut in the freezer for 5–10 minutes until firm but not frozen. Take the meat out and use a sharp knife to cut the meat into thin slices. The cooling of the meat means that it will stay firm when slicing.

 Sweet and sour pork with noodles

This looks and tastes as good as you'd get from the Chinese take away but with fewer **POINTS** values.

13 POINTS values per recipe takes 15 minutes to prepare, 10 minutes to cook

Serves 2. 457 calories per serving. Freeze ✗

100 g (3¹/2 oz) egg noodles
low fat cooking spray
1 garlic clove, crushed
200 g (7 oz) lean pork loin steak, cut in 5 cm (2 inch) batons
200 g (7 oz) baby sweetcorn, quartered lengthways
6 spring onions, chopped into 2.5 cm (1 inch) lengths
1 red and 1 yellow pepper, de-seeded and sliced thinly
100 g (3¹/2 oz) canned pineapple rings in juice, chopped
150 ml (¹/4 pint) pineapple juice
1 cm (¹/2 inch) piece of fresh root ginger, peeled and grated
2 tablespoons soy sauce
2 teaspoons cornflour

● Cook the noodles as directed on the packet, then drain.
● Meanwhile, heat a large non stick frying pan or wok until very hot. Spray with the low fat cooking spray and then stir fry the garlic and pork for 4 minutes, or until the pork is browned all over.
● Add the baby sweetcorn, spring onions, peppers and pineapple pieces and stir fry for a further 2 minutes.
● Add all the other ingredients (except the cornflour), along with the noodles, and bring to the boil. Meanwhile, mix the cornflour with 2 tablespoons of water until smooth and then add to the stir fry and stir together.
● Cook for a few minutes until the sauce thickens and then serve immediately.

(6) **Pasta primavera**

Primavera means spring in Italian and this pasta recipe is full of the joys of spring. Serve with steamed vegetables of your choice, such as asparagus or broccoli.

Ⓥ *24¹/2 POINTS values per recipe* takes 15 minutes

Serves 4. 470 calories per serving. Freeze ✗

    350 g (12 oz) dried pasta shapes
    low fat cooking spray
    2 garlic cloves, sliced finely
    a bunch of spring onions, sliced
    200 g (7 oz) frozen petits pois, defrosted
    200 g (7 oz) sugar snap peas
    300 g (10¹/2 oz) baby carrots, trimmed
    200 g (7 oz) very low fat soft cheese with garlic and herbs
    a small bunch of fresh mint, chopped
    salt and freshly ground black pepper

● Cook the pasta in plenty of boiling, salted water, in a large saucepan, for 6–8 minutes or according to the pack instructions. Drain and replace in the pan.

● Meanwhile, spray a wok or large frying pan with the low fat cooking spray. Stir fry the garlic over a medium heat until golden. Add all the vegetables and continue to stir fry for a few minutes.

● Add the soft cheese and mint to the vegetables and gently stir in; then heat through. Add the vegetable mixture to the pasta, toss together, season and serve.

 (3) **Tabbouleh**

This is a **lovely summery,** light salad, which originates in the Middle East and is traditionally served on a cos lettuce leaf, as a starter. Serve it with a Greek salad.

Ⓥ *6¹/2 POINTS values per recipe* takes 15 minutes

Serves 2. 280 calories per serving. Freeze ✗

    125 g (4¹/2 oz) bulgur wheat
    boiling water, to cover
    2 spring onions, chopped
    2 plum tomatoes, diced
    ¹/4 cucumber, diced
    2 tablespoons chopped fresh mint
    3 tablespoons chopped fresh parsley
    juice of ¹/2 lemon
    1 teaspoon whole grain mustard
    salt and freshly ground black pepper

● Place the bulgur wheat in a bowl and pour over enough boiling water just to cover. Leave to soak for 15 minutes. Mix around with a fork to break up any lumps.

● Mix in all the remaining ingredients and serve.

How to •••

make a Greek salad.

*Mix together ¹/2 a cucumber, diced, 4 ripe tomatoes, cut into wedges, 6 olives, stoned and diced, and 1 small red onion, cut into wedges. Add 100 g (3¹/2 oz) feta cheese, diced, and then sprinkle over ¹/2 teaspoon of oregano and the juice and zest of ¹/2 a lemon. This serves 2 at a **POINTS** value of 4¹/2 per serving.*

 **Chilli crusted lamb cutlets**

41½ POINTS values per recipe takes 25 minutes

Serves 4. 505 calories per serving. Freeze ✗

- 3 large red chillies, de-seeded and chopped
- 2 spring onions, chopped
- 3 tablespoons lemon juice
- 2 tablespoons chopped fresh coriander
- 8 lamb cutlets
- salt and freshly ground black pepper

For the raita

- ¼ cucumber, grated
- 200 g (7 fl oz) low fat natural yogurt
- 1 chopped fresh tablespoon mint

- Preheat the grill. Process the chillies, spring onions, lemon juice and coriander in a food processor until roughly chopped.
- Spread the mixture over both sides of the cutlets. Season well. Place the cutlets on a baking tray and cook under a hot grill for 3–4 minutes on each side or until cooked to your liking.
- Mix the raita ingredients together and serve with the cutlets.

Chilli and bacon pasta

A fiery pasta dish that takes just 15 minutes. Serve with a large zero salad.

36 POINTS values per recipe takes 20 minutes

Serves 4. 499 calories per serving. Freeze ❄ for up to 1 month

- 450 g (1 lb) tagliatelle
- low fat cooking spray
- 2 red chillies, de-seeded and chopped finely
- 8 rashers of rindless smoked lean back bacon, chopped
- 325 g (11½ oz) low fat fromage frais
- 2 tablespoons fresh shredded basil
- salt and freshly ground black pepper

- Cook the tagliatelle in a large pan of boiling salted water for 10 minutes or until al dente.
- Heat the low fat cooking spray in a frying pan and add the chillies and bacon. Cook for 5–6 minutes or until the bacon is crispy.
- Drain the pasta and return to the pan with the chilli, bacon, fromage frais, basil and seasoning. Toss together and serve immediately.

4½ POINTS VALUE **Lemon chicken and couscous salad**

This makes a great summer picnic dish.

18½ POINTS values per recipe takes 20 minutes cooking + cooling

Serves 4. 396 calories per serving. Freeze ❄ for up to 1 month

- 250 g (9 oz) couscous
- 300 ml (10 fl oz) chicken stock
- 2 cm (¾ inch) piece of fresh ginger, peeled and grated
- 1 red pepper, de-seeded and halved
- 1 yellow pepper, de-seeded and halved
- 1 courgette, grated
- 1 small carrot, grated
- 1 tablespoon chopped fresh mint
- 2 tablespoons chopped fresh coriander
- juice and rind of 1 lemon
- 2 cooked chicken breasts, shredded
- salt and freshly ground black pepper
- 75 g (2¾ oz) watercress or salad leaves, to serve

● Place the couscous in a bowl and pour over the hot stock. Cover with a clean tea towel and leave to rest for 10–15 minutes. Add the grated ginger and stir around with a fork.

● Meanwhile, place the halves of pepper, skin side up, under a hot grill and cook until very charred. Place in a bowl and cover with clingfilm until cool enough to handle. Peel off the skin and cut into strips.

● When the couscous is cool, stir vigorously with a fork and then stir in all the other ingredients, including the peppers. Season well and serve on a bed of watercress or salad leaves.

How to ...

prepare couscous.

Place the couscous in a bowl. Pour over just enough hot water or stock to cover the couscous. Cover tightly with a clean tea towel and leave for 15 minutes. This means that no steam escapes – instead it is absorbed into the grain, leaving a lovely fluffy texture. When it is ready, remove the tea towel and fluff up the grains with a fork.

 5 POINTS VALUE **Turkey chow mein**

A twist on the take away favourite – perfect for a Friday night, whichever food plan you are following.

20 POINTS values per recipe takes 4 minutes

Serves 4. 255 calories per serving. Freeze ✗

- 2 teaspoons soy sauce
- juice of 1 lime
- 125 g (4½ oz) turkey breast meat, cut into thin strips
- 225 g (8 oz) dried medium egg noodles
- low fat cooking spray
- 3 garlic cloves, chopped finely
- 50 g (1¾ oz) mange tout, shredded
- 50 g (1¾ oz) ham, shredded
- 3 teaspoons soy sauce
- 6 spring onions, sliced
- salt and freshly ground black pepper

● Mix together the 2 teaspoons of soy sauce, the lime juice and seasoning in a small bowl. Add the turkey strips and leave to marinate for 10 minutes.

● Cook the noodles in a large pan of boiling water for 3–5 minutes. Drain and then refresh under cold water. Drain again and reserve.

● Heat a wok over a high heat with low fat cooking spray. Add the turkey strips and stir fry for about 2 minutes then transfer them to a plate. Wipe the wok clean.

● Reheat the wok with low fat cooking spray, add the garlic and stir fry for 10 seconds before adding the mange tout and ham. Stir fry for 1 minute.

● Add the noodles, soy sauce and spring onions and stir fry for 2 minutes.

● Return the turkey to the wok and stir fry for another 3–4 minutes until the turkey is cooked. Serve immediately.

Beef stroganoff for two

Great for a **romantic** dinner. Serve this rich stew with plain boiled potatoes and a **peppery** watercress or rocket and tomato salad, drizzled with balsamic vinegar.

8 POINTS values per recipe takes 25 minutes

Serves 2. 225 calories per serving. Freeze ✗

- low fat cooking spray
- 2 shallots, peeled and chopped
- 2 garlic cloves, sliced finely
- 2 rump or entrecôte steaks, each 2.5 cm (1 inch) thick and approximately 150 g (5¹⁄₂ oz), all fat removed and meat sliced thinly
- 200 g (7 oz) chestnut mushrooms, sliced
- 100 ml (3¹⁄₂ fl oz) vegetable or meat stock
- 4 tablespoons very low fat fromage frais
- salt and freshly ground black pepper

● Heat a large non stick frying pan and spray it with the low fat cooking spray. Stir fry the shallots and garlic for 5 minutes or until softened, adding a little water if necessary to prevent them from sticking.

● Add the steak and mushrooms and season. Stir fry on a high heat for 2–3 minutes, until the meat is browned all over.

● With the heat still turned up high, quickly add the stock and bubble for a few seconds, scraping up any juices stuck to the bottom of the pan with a wooden spatula. Turn the heat off, allow to cool for a minute, then stir in the fromage frais and serve.

 ## Gammon with poached egg and parsley sauce

This dish goes well with **crunchy** green vegetables and potatoes mashed with skimmed milk.

34 POINTS values per recipe takes 20 minutes

Serves 4. 332 calories per serving. Freeze ✗

- 150 g (5¹⁄₂ oz) low fat fromage frais
- 75 g (2³⁄₄ oz) low fat soft cheese
- 3 tablespoons chopped fresh parsley
- 4 gammon steaks
- 4 eggs
- salt and freshly ground black pepper

● Whisk together the fromage frais and soft cheese. Heat gently in a small pan and stir in the parsley and seasoning.

● Heat a grill to medium-high and cook the gammon steaks for 6–7 minutes on each side.

● Poach the eggs.

● Serve each gammon steak with a poached egg on top, with the parsley sauce spooned over.

How to ...

poach perfect eggs

Add 2 teaspoons of white wine vinegar to a pan of swirling boiling water. Crack the eggs into separate cups. Gently pour the eggs from the cup into the water and poach for 3 minutes.

Gammon with poached egg and parsley sauce

Tuna with spring veg sauté

6 POINTS values per recipe takes 20 minutes

Serves 4. 194 calories per serving. Freeze ✗

4 tuna steaks

3 tablespoons soy sauce

juice of 1 lemon

1 teaspoon ground ginger

low fat cooking spray

3 shallots, peeled and diced

150 g (5½ oz) green beans, trimmed

100 g (3½ oz) baby carrots, peeled

50 g (1¾ oz) baby courgettes, halved lengthways

50 g (1¾ oz) cherry tomatoes

150 ml (5 fl oz) vegetable stock

salt and freshly ground black pepper

● Place the tuna steaks in a non metallic bowl.

● Mix together the soy sauce, lemon juice, pepper and ground ginger and pour this over the tuna steaks. Cover and leave to marinate for 10–15 minutes.

● Meanwhile heat a wok or large frying pan with low fat cooking spray and add the vegetables, except the cherry tomatoes. Stir fry for 5–6 minutes until they start to brown in places.

● Add the tomatoes and pour in the vegetable stock. Cook over a very high heat so the stock is bubbling well. Season and cook for 6–8 minutes, stirring occasionally.

● Meanwhile, heat a griddle with low fat cooking spray and cook the drained tuna for 5–6 minutes on each side, depending on how well cooked you like your fish.

● Serve the tuna steaks on a bed of the vegetables with a little of the sauce poured over the top.

How to ...

sear fish.

Use a pan with a good heavy base and heat until very hot before adding the fish. Leave for 5–6 minutes without moving the fish, then turn it over and complete the cooking on the other side.

 Snappy jambalaya

A great big rice dish with **bold flavours** from the American deep South.

20½ POINTS values per recipe takes 10 minutes to prepare, 20 minutes to cook

Serves 4. 405 calories per serving. Freeze ❄ without the fish

low fat cooking spray

2 large onions, chopped

1 celery stick, chopped

1 red pepper, diced

225 g (8 oz) button mushrooms, sliced

100 g (3½ oz) lean ham, diced

400 g can of chopped tomatoes

2 bay leaves

2 garlic cloves, crushed

1 fresh red chilli, de-seeded, cored and chopped finely or
½ teaspoon dried chilli flakes

225 g (8 oz) long grain rice

700 ml (1¼ pints) chicken stock

4 x 125 g (4½ oz) red snapper fillets

a small bunch of fresh parsley, chopped, to garnish

salt and freshly ground black pepper

● Spray a large frying pan with the low fat cooking spray and fry the onions for 4 minutes until softened. Add the celery, pepper and mushrooms and stir fry for 10 minutes.

● Add the ham, tomatoes and 150 ml (¼ pint) of water, bay leaves, garlic, chilli and seasoning. Stir together and then simmer for 15 minutes.

● Add the rice and stock and simmer gently for 20 minutes, stirring every now and then, until the rice is just cooked and the sauce is almost completely absorbed.

● Meanwhile, season and grill the snapper fillets for 2–3 minutes or until golden and cooked through. Spoon the jambalaya on to serving plates or big wide bowls, top each with a snapper fillet and sprinkle with parsley.

One pot wonders

Masses of washing up can be tedious, particularly if it's been a long day or you're in the middle of something. At times like this cleaning up the kitchen can be daunting, so grabbing a take away or a ready meal is an appealing option. However, these meals are often high in fat and calories and unless you have planned ahead and factored them into your **POINTS** allowance it can be difficult to stay on track. You can create some wonderfully filling, flavoursome and satisfying meals in just one pot – stews, casseroles, stir-fries and more. So, for the sake of washing up just one dish, the recipes in this chapter are well worth a try.

Chicken saag aloo (page 53)

5 POINTS VALUE ## Sweet and sour chicken

A quick, easy and tasty dish – perfect for a mid week supper.

10 POINTS values per recipe takes 20 minutes

Serves 2. 372 calories per serving. Freeze ✗

- low fat cooking spray
- 2.5 cm (1 inch) piece of fresh root ginger, peeled and grated
- 2 garlic cloves, sliced
- 2 x 150 g (5½ oz) boneless, skinless chicken breasts, cut into bite size pieces
- 1 teaspoon Chinese five spice powder
- 200 g (7 oz) carrots, sliced thinly
- a bunch of spring onions, sliced finely
- 100 g (3½ oz) sugar snap peas or mange tout
- 300 ml (½ pint) orange juice
- 1 tablespoon honey
- 1 tablespoon rice or white wine vinegar
- 2 tablespoons soy sauce
- 1 teaspoon sesame oil
- 1 tablespoon cornflour, mixed with 2 tablespoons water
- salt and freshly ground black pepper

● Heat a large non stick frying pan or wok and spray with the low fat cooking spray. Stir fry the ginger and garlic for 2 minutes, until golden, and then add the chicken pieces. Stir fry over a high heat for 5 minutes.

● Add all the other ingredients and cook until the sauce thickens and becomes glossy. Check the seasoning and serve at once.

 3½ POINTS VALUE ## Chicken saag aloo

A simple, quick curry that takes advantage of the delicious curry pastes that you can now buy in jars. Serve with a tomato and shredded onion salad.

14½ POINTS values per recipe takes 25 minutes to prepare, 20 minutes to cook

Serves 4. 255 calories per serving. Freeze ❄

- low fat cooking spray
- 4 x 150 g (5½ oz) boneless, skinless chicken breasts, cubed
- 200 g (7 oz) small new potatoes, quartered
- 1 onion, chopped finely
- 4 garlic cloves, crushed
- 5 cm (2 inch) piece of fresh root ginger, chopped finely
- 400 g (14 oz) canned chopped tomatoes
- 300 g (10½ oz) frozen spinach
- 300 ml (½ pint) chicken stock
- 2 tablespoons tandoori or balti curry paste
- a bunch of fresh coriander, chopped
- salt and freshly ground black pepper
- lemon wedges, to serve

● Heat a large non stick frying pan and spray with the low fat cooking spray, then stir fry the chicken for 4 minutes or so until golden on the edges and white all over. Add the potatoes, onion, garlic and ginger and stir fry for a further 4 minutes.

● Add the tomatoes, spinach, stock and curry paste and bring to the boil. Simmer gently for 20 minutes, until the chicken is tender, the potatoes cooked through and the sauce thickened.

● Stir in the coriander, check the seasoning, adding more if necessary. Serve with the lemon wedges.

Garlic chicken casserole

A soothing chicken dish, **infused** with the **flavour** of garlic. Serve with mashed butternut squash.

15½ POINTS values per recipe takes 10 minutes to prepare, 1 hour to cook

Serves 6. 180 calories per serving. Freeze ✗

- **low fat cooking spray**
- **6 x 150 g (5½ oz) skinless, boneless chicken breasts**
- **3 whole heads of garlic**
- **a small bunch of thyme, woody stems removed and leaves chopped**
- **a few rosemary sprigs, woody stems removed and leaves chopped**
- **100 ml (3½ fl oz) dry white wine**
- **400 ml (14 fl oz) chicken stock**
- **salt and freshly ground black pepper**
- **a small bunch of fresh parsley, chopped, to garnish**

● Preheat the oven to Gas Mark 4/180°C/fan oven 160°C. Heat a large non stick flameproof casserole, spray with the low fat cooking spray and season; then fry the chicken breasts gently for 5–6 minutes until browned all over.

● Separate the cloves of garlic, then peel and scatter them over the top of the chicken with the herbs and seasoning. Pour over the wine and stock, cover the casserole and bake in the oven for 1 hour.

● Serve hot, sprinkled with the parsley.

How to ●●●

make a butternut squash mash.

Cut a butternut squash in half and scoop out the seeds. Cut each half into wedges and spray with low fat cooking spray. Season and place skin side down on a roasting tray. Roast at Gas Mark 7/220° C/fan oven 200°C for 20–25 minutes. When cool enough to handle, scoop out the flesh and mash with a little skimmed milk, then season.

 Pot roast chicken

Ideal for a **winter's evening** and best served with lots of green vegetables such as steamed broccoli, beans or spinach.

24 POINTS values per recipe takes 30 minutes to prepare, 20–25 minutes to cook

Serves 4. 327 calories per serving. Freeze ✗

- **low fat cooking spray**
- **4 x medium (135 g/5 oz) chicken quarters, with skin on**
- **6–8 small shallots**
- **100 ml (3½ fl oz) white wine**
- **1 litre (1¾ pints) hot chicken or vegetable stock**
- **2 tablespoons sun dried tomato paste**
- **1 teaspoon dried Mediterranean herbs, e.g. oregano, marjoram and/or basil**
- **400 g (14 oz) new potatoes, large ones quartered or halved**
- **2 large carrots, cut in 1 cm (½ inch) diagonal slices**
- **2 celery sticks, chopped**
- **salt and freshly ground black pepper**
- **a large bunch of fresh tarragon or basil, chopped, to serve**

● Heat a large non stick casserole dish, spray with the low fat cooking spray and then season and fry the chicken quarters for 10 minutes on each side, until golden all over. Add the shallots and fry for a further 10 minutes, until golden also. Add the white wine and boil rapidly, scraping up any browned juices from the base of the pan.

● Meanwhile, preheat the oven to Gas Mark 6/200°C/fan oven 180°C. Remove from the hob and add all the other ingredients except the fresh herbs. Cover and roast for 20–25 minutes until the juices run clear when the joints are stuck with a skewer in the thickest part of the thigh.

● Check the seasoning, remove the skin and serve sprinkled with the chopped tarragon or basil.

Summer vegetable casserole

Serve this **bright** and **tasty** stew with a generous portion of green beans or sugar snap peas for no extra *POINTS* values.

3½ POINTS values per recipe takes 45 minutes

Serves 2. 245 calories per serving. Freeze ✗

low fat cooking spray
1 onion, chopped
1 garlic clove, crushed
1 small aubergine, cubed
1 large red pepper, de-seeded and diced
225 g (8 oz) potatoes, cubed
2 teaspoons fennel seeds, crushed
400 g (14 oz) canned chopped tomatoes
90 ml (3¼ fl oz) dry white wine
2 courgettes, sliced
salt and freshly ground black pepper

● Heat a large saucepan, spray with the low fat cooking spray and then add the onion and garlic and stir fry for 2–3 minutes, until golden, adding a little water if necessary to prevent them from sticking.

● Add the remaining ingredients, except the courgettes, and bring to the boil. Cover and simmer for 20 minutes, until the potatoes are cooked through.

● Remove the lid, add the courgettes and simmer for a further 5 minutes until they are tender and the casserole is thick. Check the seasoning before serving.

 ## Hearty beef and beer casserole

A **rich** and **comforting** stew that is excellent with steamed leeks and a baked potato for an extra *POINTS* value of 2½.

13 POINTS values per recipe takes 30 minutes to prepare, 1 hour to cook

Serves 4. 195 calories per serving. Freeze ❄

low fat cooking spray
400 g (14 oz) lean stewing steak, cubed
2 onions, chopped finely
2 tablespoons plain flour
2 carrots, sliced finely
4 celery sticks, sliced finely
2 fresh sage sprigs, chopped (optional)
200 g (7 oz) baby button mushrooms, washed
300 ml (½ pint) beef stock
150 ml (¼ pint) beer
salt and freshly ground black pepper

● Preheat the oven to Gas Mark 2/150°C/fan oven 130°C. Heat a non stick flameproof casserole and spray with the low fat cooking spray. Season and fry the beef on a high heat, then add the onions and stir fry for a further 5 minutes. Add the flour and stir to coat the meat.

● Add the carrots, celery, sage, if using, mushrooms and seasoning and stir fry together for a minute or two, taking care not to let the flour burn.

● Pour over the stock and beer and stir, incorporating any 'stuck' juices into the gravy. Cover and place in the oven for 1 hour, stirring occasionally. If the stew starts to dry out, add a little stock or water.

3 POINTS VALUE — Sweet pumpkin and peanut curry

Serve this hearty curry with 4 tablespoons of cooked basmati rice for an extra *POINTS* value of 3 per serving.

 12½ *POINTS values per recipe* takes 30 minutes to prepare, 20 minutes to cook

Serves 4. 209 calories per serving. Freeze ✗

- **2 teaspoons vegetable oil**
- **4 garlic cloves, crushed**
- **4 shallots, chopped finely**
- **2 teaspoons red or green Thai curry paste**
- **600 ml (1 pint) vegetable stock**
- **2 lime leaves, torn**
- **2.5 cm (1 inch) piece of fresh root ginger, peeled and chopped finely**
- **450 g (1 lb) pumpkin, peeled, de-seeded and cubed**
- **200 g (7 oz) sweet potatoes, peeled and cubed**
- **100 g (3½ oz) mushrooms, sliced**
- **100 ml (3½ fl oz) low fat coconut milk**
- **50 g (1¾ oz) roasted peanuts, chopped**
- **3 tablespoons soy sauce**
- **a small bunch of fresh coriander, chopped**

● Heat the oil in a large non stick pan and then fry the garlic and shallots for 10 minutes, until softened and golden, adding a little water if necessary to prevent them from sticking. Add the curry paste and stir fry for 30 seconds. Then add the stock, lime leaves, ginger, pumpkin and sweet potatoes. Bring to the boil, and then simmer for 20 minutes or until the potatoes are cooked.
● Add the mushrooms and simmer for 5 minutes more before removing from the heat and stirring in the coconut milk, peanuts, soy sauce and coriander. Serve.

How to ●●●

prepare the pumpkin.

Cut the pumpkin into wedges and then remove the flesh in large sections with a sharp knife. Alternatively, cut the pumpkin into strips and remove the rind with a potato peeler before cutting into chunks.

6½ POINTS VALUE — Sicilian aubergine stew with polenta

 27 *POINTS values per recipe* takes 25 minutes to prepare, 20 minutes to cook

Serves 4. 498 calories per serving. Freeze ❄

- **low fat cooking spray**
- **1 large onion, chopped**
- **2 garlic cloves, chopped**
- **4 celery sticks, chopped**
- **2 aubergines, cubed**
- **400 g (14 oz) canned chopped tomatoes**
- **2 tablespoons tomato purée**
- **3 tablespoons red wine vinegar**
- **2 teaspoons sugar**
- **2 tablespoons raisins**
- **2 tablespoons capers**
- **20 stoned black or green olives, sliced**
- **25 g (1 oz) pine nut kernels**
- **400 g (14 oz) instant polenta**
- **300 ml (½ pint) vegetable stock**
- **salt and freshly ground black pepper**
- **a small bunch of fresh parsley, chopped**

● Heat a large non stick saucepan and spray with the low fat cooking spray. Add the onion and garlic and fry for 2–3 minutes, until softened, adding a little water if necessary to prevent them from sticking.
● Add the celery, aubergines, tomatoes, tomato purée, red wine vinegar, sugar, raisins, capers, olives and seasoning and bring to the boil.
● Simmer, covered, for 20 minutes, stirring frequently, and then stir in the pine nut kernels.
● Meanwhile, make up the polenta with the stock as directed on the packet. Serve the stew with the polenta, scattered with the chopped parsley.

(3 POINTS VALUE) Fish stew

A **soupy stew**, thickened with floury potatoes. Serve in big bowls, with **crusty rolls**. A medium (50 g/1¾ oz) roll has a *POINTS* value of 2.

17½ POINTS values per recipe takes 20 minutes to prepare, 35 minutes to cook

Serves 6. 239 calories per serving. Freeze ✗

  2 teaspoons olive oil
  2 onions, sliced
  450 g (1 lb) pumpkin or butternut squash, peeled, de-seeded
      and cut in small cubes
  1 litre (1¾ pints) chicken or vegetable stock
  450 g (1 lb) floury potatoes
  200 ml (7 fl oz) dry white wine
  250 g (9 oz) frozen sweetcorn
  300 g (10½ oz) smoked haddock fillet, skinned and cut in chunks
  300 g (10½ oz) haddock fillet, skinned and cut in chunks
  a bunch of watercress, shredded (reserve a few sprigs for garnish)
  salt and freshly ground black pepper
  Tabasco sauce, to serve

● In a large non stick saucepan, heat the oil and gently fry the onions for 5 minutes or until soft, adding a little water if necessary to prevent them from sticking.
● Add the pumpkin or butternut squash, stock, potatoes and wine, bring to the boil and then simmer for 30 minutes, or until the potatoes have broken up and thickened the stew.
● Add the sweetcorn together with both kinds of fish and the watercress. Bring back to just below boiling and simmer very gently for 5 minutes; then season and serve in soup plates or bowls with a dash of Tabasco.

 (7½ POINTS VALUE) Prawn and tomato curry

A **warming**, spicy curry that is so easy to make – just one pan does it all!

29½ POINTS values per recipe takes 35 minutes

Serves 4. 507 calories per serving. Freeze ❄ for up to 1 month

  400 g can of chopped tomatoes
  1 medium onion, diced
  1 garlic clove, chopped
  4 tablespoons chopped, fresh coriander
  100 g (3½ oz) frozen peas
  200 ml (7 fl oz) fish stock
  1 teaspoon ground coriander
  2 teaspoons ground cumin
  2 tablespoons tomato purée
  400 g (14 oz) brown or long grain rice
  1.2 litres (2 pints) vegetable stock
  ½ teaspoon ground turmeric
  1 teaspoon ground cumin
  500 g (1 lb 2 oz) tiger prawns
  4 tablespoons low fat fromage frais
  salt and freshly ground black pepper

● Place the tomatoes, onion, garlic, half the chopped coriander, peas and stock into a saucepan and simmer for 5 minutes.
● Mix the spices with the tomato purée and add to the tomato mixture in the pan. Simmer for another 5 minutes.
● Meanwhile place the rice, stock and spices in a large saucepan, bring to the boil and simmer for 6–8 minutes until the rice is cooked.
● Add the prawns, simmer for 2 minutes before stirring in the fromage frais and remaining chopped coriander.
● Season the curry well and serve with the drained spicy rice.

One pot wonders

 3 POINTS VALUE **Star anise beef stew**

Here is an Asian idea of a stew – more of a **fragrant** soup with **tender** morsels of beef. Serve with 4 tablespoons of cooked rice for an extra *POINTS* value of 3 per serving.

12 POINTS values per recipe takes 15 minutes to prepare, 30 minutes to cook

Serves 4. 173 calories per serving. Freeze ✗

- 1 litre (1¾ pints) vegetable or chicken stock
- 450 g (1 lb) beef steak, cut into thin slivers
- 3 garlic cloves, chopped finely
- 2 cinnamon sticks
- 4 star anise
- 3 tablespoons soy sauce
- 1 teaspoon artificial sweetener
- 125 g (4 oz) beansprouts
- 1 spring onion, chopped finely
- a small bunch of coriander, chopped roughly

● Put the stock in a large saucepan with the beef, garlic, cinnamon, star anise, soy and sweetener. Bring to the boil and simmer for 30 minutes, skimming any scum off the top occasionally.

● In the meantime, put the beansprouts into the bottom of four serving bowls. Ladle the hot soup over the beansprouts and garnish with the spring onion and coriander.

How to •••

cook the perfect rice.

In a saucepan place 1 part rice to 2 parts cold water with a sprinkling of salt to draw out the flavour. Bring to the boil then reduce the heat, cover and cook until little steam holes appear in the rice. Remove the lid and fluff up the rice with a fork.

 3½ POINTS VALUE **Chicken korma**

14 POINTS values per recipe takes 20 minutes to prepare, 55 minutes to cook

Serves 4. 380 calories per serving. Freeze ❄ for up to 1 month

- 6 garlic cloves, peeled and chopped
- 4 cm (1½ inch) piece fresh ginger, peeled and chopped
- 2 tablespoons chicken stock
- low fat cooking spray
- 1 onion, diced finely
- 1 bay leaf
- 8 cardamom pods, cracked
- 4 cloves
- 2.5 cm (1 inch) cinnamon stick
- 1 tablespoon ground cumin
- 1 tablespoon ground coriander
- ¼ teaspoon cayenne pepper
- 1 tablespoon tomato purée
- 4 x chicken breasts, cut into bite size pieces
- 3 tablespoons low fat fromage frais
- 3 tablespoons low fat natural yogurt
- 150 ml (5 fl oz) chicken stock
- 2 teaspoons garam masala

● Place the garlic, ginger and chicken stock into a blender and blend to a paste.

● Heat a large non stick frying pan with the low fat cooking spray and add the onion, bay leaf, cardamom, cloves and cinnamon stick. Cook for 3–4 minutes, stirring occasionally.

● Add the ground cumin and coriander, cayenne pepper and tomato purée. Stir to combine. Stir in the chicken to coat with all the spices.

● Stir in the remaining ingredients and bring to a simmer for 25 minutes or until the chicken is cooked through.

Fruity chicken curry

A fruity, **great tasting** curry that goes well with plain, boiled rice.

10½ POINTS values per recipe takes 20 minutes to prepare, 20 minutes to cook

Serves 4. 278 calories per serving. Freeze ❄ for up to 1 month

> low fat cooking spray
> 100 g (3½ oz) bacon lardons
> 1 onion, chopped
> 4 chicken breasts (approx 165 g/5¾ oz each), cut into
>   bite size pieces
> 1 teaspoon curry powder
> 1 teaspoon ground cumin
> 1 apple, cored and sliced
> 1 banana, sliced
> 4 plum tomatoes, chopped
> 250 ml (9 fl oz) chicken stock

● Heat a large saucepan with low fat cooking spray and add the bacon lardons and onion. Cook for 2–3 minutes before adding the chicken.

● Brown the chicken and then sprinkle in the spices. Stir to coat the chicken.

● Add the remaining ingredients and bring to a simmer. Simmer for 15–20 minutes and serve.

 Spicy vegetable chilli

This is a **wonderfully colourful** dish, with lots of crunchiness and flavour.

Ⓥ *6 POINTS values per recipe* takes 15 minutes to prepare, 20 minutes to cook

Serves 4. 165 calories per serving. Freeze ❄ for up to 1 month

> low fat cooking spray
> 1 onion, chopped
> 1 garlic clove, crushed
> 2 red peppers, de-seeded and chopped
> 1 teaspoon chilli powder
> 2 carrots, diced
> 150 g (5½ oz) frozen sweetcorn
> 400 g can of kidney beans, drained and rinsed
> 1 x 400 g can of chopped tomatoes
> shredded iceberg lettuce, to serve

● Heat a large saucepan with low fat cooking spray. Fry the onion for 2–3 minutes until starting to soften.

● Add the garlic and peppers and cook for another 4–5 minutes.

● Stir in the chilli powder then add the remaining ingredients.

● Simmer for 20 minutes. Serve on a bed of shredded iceberg lettuce.

Apple and pork braise

This easy dish has a real **autumnal** feel to it. Serve with mashed or baked potatoes and roasted parsnips.

19 POINTS values per recipe takes 30 minutes to prepare, 25 minutes to cook
Serves 4. 154 calories per serving. Freeze ✗

- low fat cooking spray
- 400 g (14 oz) pork leg steaks, trimmed of all fat and diced into bite size pieces
- 2 small onions, chopped
- 2 garlic cloves, crushed
- 4 celery stalks, chopped finely
- a small bunch of fresh sage, chopped, but reserve a few small whole leaves to garnish
- 450 g (1 lb) cooking apples, peeled, cored and chopped
- 300 ml (1/2 pint) vegetable stock
- salt and freshly ground black pepper

● Heat a large non stick frying pan and spray with low fat cooking spray, then stir fry the pork for a few minutes until browned on all sides.

● Add the onions and garlic and stir fry for another 5 minutes, until softened, adding a little water if necessary to prevent them from sticking.

● Add the celery, sage, apples, stock and seasoning. Bring to the boil, then cover and simmer for 25 minutes. Serve garnished with the reserved sage leaves.

How to ...

braise meat.
Place the meat in a large frying pan with a little low fat cooking spray on a low temperature. Fry the meat with any 'marinade' ingredients such as garlic and onion, allowing the meat to gently combine with the flavours. Add a little water or liquid and then simmer gently to draw out the flavours.

 ## One pan turkey Bolognese

A **healthy twist** on the usual spaghetti Bolognese – and all cooked in just one pot.

41/2 POINTS values per recipe takes 25 minutes
Serves 1. 395 calories per serving. Freeze ✗

- low fat cooking spray
- 1 small onion, chopped finely
- 1 clove garlic, crushed
- 100 g (31/2 oz) turkey mince
- 100 ml (31/2 fl oz) chicken stock
- 1 teaspoon tomato puree
- 1 teaspoon soy sauce
- 1 x 200 g can chopped tomatoes
- 50 g dried spaghetti, broken into short lengths
- 100 g (31/2 oz) mixed zero vegetables, chopped finely
- salt and freshly ground black pepper

● Heat a non stick saucepan and spray with the low fat cooking spray, then stir fry the onion and garlic for a few minutes until softened, adding a few tablespoons of the stock if necessary to prevent them from sticking.

● Add the turkey mince, season and stir fry for a further 3 minutes until it is browned and crumbly. Add all the other ingredients except for the vegetables and bring to the boil. Reduce the heat and simmer, covered, for 10 minutes.

● Add the vegetables and stir in, then simmer uncovered for 5 minutes more and serve.

Paella

A great **party** dish – lots of **lovely seafood** cooked with delicious flavoured rice.

31 POINTS values per recipe takes 35 minutes

Serves 6. 489 calories per serving. Freeze ✗

- **low fat cooking spray**
- **1 large Spanish onion, chopped**
- **2 garlic cloves, chopped**
- **225 g (8 oz) long grain rice**
- **1 litre (1³/4 pints) fish stock**
- **a pinch of saffron**
- **16 langoustines**
- **450 g (1 lb) live mussels, cleaned**
- **10 scallops**
- **125 g (4¹/2 oz) crabsticks**
- **500 g (1 lb 2 oz) shell on prawns**
- **400 g (14 oz) cooked chicken, chopped**
- **400 g can of chopped tomatoes**
- **salt and freshly ground black pepper**

● Heat the low fat cooking spray in a large frying pan or paella pan if you have one.

● Add the onion and cook until soft. Add the garlic and rice and cook, stirring, for 2–3 minutes.

● Add the stock to the pan, cover and cook very slowly for 10–15 minutes or until the rice is nearly cooked – add a little water if the rice begins to stick.

● Add the saffron to the pan with the mussels and scallops. Cook for another 3–4 minutes until the mussel shells have opened.

● Stir in the crabsticks, prawns, chicken and tomatoes and cook for a further 4–5 minutes. Season well and serve immediately.

 Lentil and vegetable stew

This **hearty**, warming stew can be served with a chunky jacket potato for a really **filling** winter meal.

Ⓥ *5¹/2 POINTS values per recipe* takes 10 minutes to prepare + soaking, 45–50 minutes to cook

Serves 4. 118 calories per serving. Freeze ❄ for up to 1 month

- **100 g (3¹/2 oz) green lentils, soaked in water for 2 hours**
- **300 ml (¹/2 pint) vegetable stock**
- **¹/2 onion, chopped**
- **¹/2 red pepper, sliced**
- **1 carrot, halved lengthways and sliced**
- **1 potato, chopped**
- **50 g (1³/4 oz) broccoli, broken into florets**
- **75 g (2³/4 oz) mushrooms, sliced**
- **salt and freshly ground black pepper**
- **1 tablespoon chopped fresh parsley, to serve**

● Cook the soaked lentils over a gentle heat in the vegetable stock for 30 minutes.

● Add the remaining ingredients and simmer for 15–20 minutes or until the vegetables are tender. Serve sprinkled with chopped parsley.

How to ●●●

prepare lentils.

First pick over the lentils to remove any pieces of grit and any discoloured lentils. Rinse the lentils in cold water, discarding any that float. Place the lentils in a large pan and cover with a generous amount of cold water. Leave to soak for 1–2 hours before using.

On a budget

There are few of us who have the luxury of being able to spend whatever we want, whenever we want. Most of us have times when things are a little tight and we have to rein in our spending. When this happens, the challenge is to get more creative about how we spend our money. The same principle applies to food. With a touch of inspiration and some wise food choices you really can make the most of your meals. In fact, by getting to grips with foods and their flavours, you can create delicious meals from the most basic store cupboard ingredients. Even if you have friends for dinner, there's no need to spend a huge amount on expensive ingredients – just take a look through this chapter for some inspiring ideas on how to make your money go further.

Potato and courgette gratin (page 71)

[creative]

7 POINTS VALUE
Sticky cranberry gammon

7 POINTS values per recipe takes 30 minutes

Serves 1. 367 calories per serving. Freeze ✗

150 g (5½ oz) lean gammon steak, all fat removed

1 teaspoon honey

50 g (1¾ oz) frozen or fresh cranberries

2 teaspoons whole grain mustard

50 g (1¾ oz) mange tout or sugar snap peas

50 g (1¾ oz) green beans

50 g (1¾ oz) peas

salt and freshly ground black pepper

● Preheat the grill to high and lay the gammon steak on the grill pan. In a small, covered saucepan, heat the honey with the cranberries, 1 teaspoon of the mustard, seasoning and 2 tablespoons of water. Cook for about 3–4 minutes, until the cranberries start to pop.

● Brush the gammon steak with the cranberry mixture and grill for 5–6 minutes on each side, brushing frequently with the cranberry mixture.

● Meanwhile, blanch the vegetables for 30 seconds in salted, boiling water and then toss with the remaining teaspoon of mustard and seasoning.

● Serve the gammon with the vegetables and any remaining sauce poured over.

 5½ POINTS VALUE
Spaghetti Bolognese

This is a low **POINTS** value version of the Italian classic and is perfect for sharing with family or friends. Enjoy accompanied by a 175 ml glass of red wine for an extra **POINTS** value of 2.

22½ POINTS values per recipe takes 35 minutes

Serves 4. 431 calories per serving. Freeze ❄ sauce only

low fat cooking spray

2 onions, chopped finely

2 garlic cloves, chopped finely

300 g (10½ oz) extra lean beef mince

2 carrots, chopped finely

2 celery sticks, chopped finely

400 g can of chopped tomatoes

2 tablespoons tomato purée

leaves from 2 fresh thyme sprigs or 1 teaspoon dried thyme

100 ml (3½ fl oz) red wine

2 tablespoons Worcestershire sauce

225 g (8 oz) dried spaghetti

a small bunch of fresh parsley, chopped

salt and freshly ground black pepper

● Spray a large frying pan with the low fat cooking spray and put on a medium heat. Fry the onions and garlic for about 5 minutes or until softened. Add the mince, breaking it up with the back of a wooden spoon, and cook until it is browned all over.

● Add the carrots, celery, tomatoes, tomato purée, thyme, seasoning, red wine and Worcestershire sauce. Stir together and leave to simmer for 30 minutes.

● Meanwhile, cook the spaghetti in plenty of boiling, salted water for 10 minutes. Drain and add to the sauce.

● Season to taste. Stir in the parsley before serving.

4 POINTS VALUE Bubble and squeak pie

This is a great dish if you have leftovers from a roast dinner and it is **so tasty**.

17 POINTS values per recipe takes 15 minutes to prepare, 25–30 minutes to cook

Serves 4. 208 calories per serving. Freeze ✗

low fat cooking spray

200 g (7 oz) roast beef, chopped finely

450 g (1 lb) cooked, leftover zero vegetables, e.g. carrots, cabbage and green beans, chopped roughly

400 g (14 oz) cooked potatoes, mashed without fat

2 tablespoons Worcestershire sauce

1 tablespoon tomato ketchup

a small bunch of fresh parsley, chopped (optional)

50 g (1¾ oz) half fat mature Cheddar cheese, grated

salt and freshly ground black pepper

● Preheat the oven to Gas Mark 4/180°C/fan oven 160°C and spray a large baking dish with the low fat cooking spray.

● In a large bowl, mix together all the ingredients except the cheese, season and pile into the baking dish. Sprinkle with the cheese and bake for 25–30 minutes until heated through and golden on top.

5 POINTS VALUE Potato and courgette gratin

Ⓥ *21 POINTS values per recipe* takes 20 minutes to prepare, 1 hour to cook

Serves 4. 381 calories per serving. Freeze ✗

low fat cooking spray

450 g (1 lb) large potatoes, grated finely, rinsed and drained

8 courgettes, grated

a small bunch of thyme, chopped (optional)

50 g (1¾ oz) polyunsaturated margarine

50 g (1¾ oz) plain flour

600 ml (1 pint) skimmed milk

100 g (3½ oz) low fat soft cheese

1 tablespoon French mustard

4 tomatoes, sliced

25 g (1 oz) half fat mature Cheddar cheese, grated

salt and freshly ground black pepper

● Preheat the oven to Gas Mark 4/180°C/fan oven 160°C. Spray a large gratin dish or casserole with the low fat cooking spray.

● Mix together the potatoes, courgettes and thyme, (if using, and reserving a little to garnish) and pile into the gratin dish in layers.

● Melt the margarine in a saucepan and add the flour. Stir for a few minutes and then add the milk gradually, stirring between additions to make a smooth sauce.

● Add the soft cheese, mustard and seasoning and pour this sauce over the vegetables, then fold together. Arrange the tomato slices over the top and sprinkle over the grated Cheddar cheese. Cook for 1 hour; cover with foil for the first 30 minutes.

How to ...

make a white sauce.

Melt a little margarine on a low heat. Sift in the same quantity of plain flour and stir gradually until you get a smooth paste. Add the milk very slowly, stirring vigorously with every new addition. Keep adding the milk until you get a smooth, thick sauce.

Beef burgers

These home made burgers are easy to make and much more delicious than their shop bought counterparts. Serve on medium burger buns with lots of salad for an extra *POINTS* value of 2.

12¹/₂ POINTS values per recipe takes 35 minutes

Serves 4. 200 calories per serving. Freeze ✗

250 g (9 oz) extra lean beef mince

2 courgettes, grated

1 carrot, grated

1 large onion, grated

2 garlic cloves, crushed

1 red pepper, de-seeded and chopped

2 teaspoons English mustard

2 slices of bread, made into breadcrumbs

1 egg

low fat cooking spray

salt and freshly ground black pepper

For the spicy salsa

¹/₂ cucumber, chopped finely

¹/₂ small red onion, chopped finely

1 red chilli, de-seeded and chopped finely

¹/₂ teaspoon caster sugar

2 tablespoons rice vinegar or white wine vinegar

● Mix all the ingredients for the burgers together (except the low fat cooking spray) and then take tablespoons of the mixture and mould into eight burgers.

● Spray a frying pan with the low fat cooking spray and fry the burgers in batches for about 3–4 minutes on each side or until cooked through.

● Put them on a plate, cover with foil and keep warm while you cook the others.

● Meanwhile, make the salsa by mixing all the ingredients together with seasoning.

● Serve the burgers with the salsa.

 Pasta with sausage and mustard sauce

A lovely, easy meal that is sure to warm and soothe on an autumnal evening. Serve with roasted red peppers tossed with garlic, balsamic vinegar and seasoning for no extra *POINTS* values.

Ⓨ *if you use vegetarian sausages 28¹/₂ POINTS values per recipe* takes 35 minutes to prepare, 15 minutes to cook

Serves 4. 404 calories per serving. Freeze ✗

175 g (6 oz) spaghetti

low fat cooking spray

2 garlic cloves, chopped finely

400 g (14 oz) low fat sausages, sliced diagonally

100 ml (3¹/₂ fl oz) white wine

100 ml (3¹/₂ fl oz) vegetable stock

2 tablespoons Dijon or wholegrain mustard

85 g bag of watercress or baby spinach, shredded

4 tablespoons half fat crème fraîche

a small bunch of fresh parsley, thyme or oregano, tough stems removed, leaves chopped, plus extra to garnish

salt and freshly ground black pepper

● Cook the pasta in plenty of boiling, salted water for 5 minutes or according to the instructions on the packet, until al dente.

● While this is cooking, heat a large, non stick frying pan, spray with the low fat cooking spray and then stir fry the garlic for 30 seconds. Add the sausages and stir fry on a medium heat for 5–10 minutes, until they are browned all over.

● Turn up the heat, add the wine and then bubble for a few seconds before adding the stock, mustard and watercress or baby spinach, mix thoroughly and then simmer for 5 minutes. Turn off the heat and stir in the crème fraîche and herbs.

● Drain the pasta but retain a little of the cooking liquid and add it to the sauce. This will help the sauce to stick to the pasta. Toss it all together, season and serve. Garnish with the reserved herb of your choice.

3 POINTS VALUE

Mushroom ragu

A creamy mushroom sauce that makes a tasty accompaniment to pasta, baked potato, meat or fish.

 6 POINTS values per recipe takes 15 minutes to prepare, 15–20 minutes to cook

Serves 2. 191 calories per serving. Freeze ✗

- low fat cooking spray
- 2 garlic cloves, crushed
- 400 g (14 oz) mushrooms, cleaned
- 100 ml (3½ fl oz) white wine
- 400 g can of chopped tomatoes
- 100 g (3½ oz) half fat crème fraîche
- a small bunch of fresh parsley or thyme, chopped
- salt and freshly ground black pepper

● Heat a large non stick frying pan and spray with the low fat cooking spray. Fry the garlic for 1 minute. Add the mushrooms and stir fry for 2–3 minutes.

● Add the seasoning, wine and tomatoes. Bring to the boil and then reduce the heat to a gentle simmer.

● Cook for a further 15–20 minutes, until the ragu is thick. Turn off the heat and stir in the crème fraîche and parsley or thyme.

5 POINTS VALUE

Turkey, ham and sweetcorn pie

This cheesy potato topped pie is a great hit with adults and children.

29 POINTS values per recipe takes 40 minutes to prepare, 30 minutes to cook

Serves 6. 323 calories per serving. Freeze ✗

- 900 g (2 lb) potatoes, peeled
- 600 ml (1 pint) skimmed milk
- low fat cooking spray
- 450 g (1 lb) turkey steaks, chopped into bite size pieces
- 1 onion, sliced
- 200 g (7 oz) frozen sweetcorn
- 150 g (5½ oz) thick sliced lean ham, diced
- 2 tablespoons plain flour
- 1 tablespoon wholegrain mustard
- a small bunch of fresh parsley, chopped
- 25 g (1 oz) half fat mature Cheddar cheese
- salt and freshly ground black pepper

● Boil the potatoes in plenty of salted water for 25 minutes, until tender, then drain and mash with seasoning and 4 tablespoons of the milk.

● Meanwhile, preheat the oven to Gas Mark 6/200°C/fan oven 180°C. Heat a large non stick frying pan and spray with the low fat cooking spray. Add the turkey and seasoning and stir fry for 4–5 minutes. Remove to a plate.

● Spray the pan again and add the onion. Stir fry for 5 minutes until softened, adding a little water if necessary to stop them sticking, then add the sweetcorn and ham and season. Cook for a further 4 minutes on a high heat.

● Put the turkey pieces back in the pan with the sweetcorn mixture, add the flour and stir together, then add the rest of the milk. Stir and scrape up any juices stuck to the bottom of the pan. Keep stirring vigorously until you have a thick, smooth sauce.

● Stir in the mustard and chopped parsley. Pour the mixture into an ovenproof dish and top with the mashed potato. Grate over the cheese and bake for 30 minutes, until crisp on top.

Burritos with petit pois guacamole

This simple supper dish is very filling. Serve with watercress or a mixed leaf salad.

Ⓨ *5 POINTS values per recipe* takes 30 minutes

Serves 1. 468 calories per serving. Freeze ✗

1 red pepper, halved and de-seeded

low fat cooking spray

1 small red onion, chopped finely

1 garlic clove, crushed

150 g (5½ oz) mushrooms, halved

100 g (3½ oz) canned red kidney beans, drained, rinsed
   and mashed

juice of ½ lemon

1 large flour tortilla

salt and freshly ground black pepper

For the guacamole

50 g (1¾ oz) frozen petits pois, cooked and drained

juice of ½ lemon

half a tablespoon of low fat yogurt

50 g (1¾) cherry tomatoes, chopped

½ shallot, chopped finely

15 g (½ oz) half fat mature Cheddar cheese, grated

● Preheat the grill to high. Grill the pepper, skin side up, until charred and blistered. Place in a plastic bag, twist the top and leave until cool enough to handle.

● Meanwhile, heat a large non stick frying pan, spray with the low fat cooking spray and then stir fry the onion and garlic for 5 minutes, or until softened, adding a little water if necessary to prevent them from sticking.

● Skin and chop the pepper. Add to the pan, with the mushrooms, kidney beans, lemon juice and seasoning.

● Spoon into the centre of the tortilla, fold over the ends and roll up to make a parcel. Place in a baking dish.

● Place the peas in a food processor with the lemon juice, yogurt and seasoning. Blend to a purée or mash with a fork. Fold in the tomatoes and shallot and spoon on top of the tortilla. Preheat the grill to high.

● Sprinkle the grated cheese over the top and grill for 2–3 minutes, until the cheese is melted and golden.

Smoked haddock kedgeree

A classic recipe using smoked haddock, this kedgeree is tasty and substantial. If you keep some smoked haddock fillets in the freezer, try the kedgeree for an impromptu Sunday brunch or quick supper standby.

19½ POINTS values per recipe takes 20 minutes to prepare, 30–35 minutes to cook

Serves 4. 393 calories per serving. Freeze ✗

300 g (10½ oz) smoked haddock fillets

2 bay leaves

4 whole peppercorns

300 ml (½ pint) skimmed milk

low fat cooking spray

2 onions, chopped

225 g (8 oz) basmati rice

a pinch of saffron threads, soaked in 2 tablespoons boiling water
    for 2 minutes

1 tablespoon garam masala

700 ml (1¼ pints) chicken or vegetable stock

a large bunch of fresh parsley, chopped finely, stalks included

200 g (7 oz) very low fat plain fromage frais

salt and freshly ground black pepper

2 eggs, hard boiled and quartered, to garnish

1 lemon, cut into wedges, to garnish

- Place the haddock fillets skin side up in a large pan with the bay leaves and peppercorns. Pour over the milk and bring to the boil; then turn off and leave to cool.

- Meanwhile, heat a large non stick frying pan or wok and spray with the low fat cooking spray. Fry the onions until golden and softened, adding a little water if necessary to prevent them from sticking.

- Add the rice, saffron threads with their soaking water and the garam masala, stirring to mix. Then add the stock and bring to the boil, stirring occasionally. Turn down to a gentle simmer and leave to cook for 15 minutes.

- Remove the haddock from the milk and flake with your fingers on to a plate, removing the skin and any bones you find as you go. Strain the milk, add it to the rice and stir in.

- After about 15–20 minutes, when the rice is just cooked and most of the liquid absorbed, add the flaked haddock, parsley and fromage frais. Stir to heat through. Check the seasoning and, serve garnished with the egg and lemon wedges.

How to ●●●

get the perfect hard boiled egg.

Try to always use an egg that is at room temperature, rather than one straight from the fridge. Place the eggs in a small saucepan and add enough cold water to just cover them. Slowly bring the water to simmering point and let the eggs cook for about 7–8 minutes. Gently take the eggs out of the pan and run cold water over them before allowing them to rest in cold water for a couple of minutes.

Smoked haddock kedgeree

4 POINTS VALUE

French ham and bean casserole

This is a **quick** and **satisfying** stew for a cold night. Serve with spinach and mashed potatoes.

4 POINTS values per recipe takes 25 minutes

Serves 1. 327 calories per serving. Freeze ✗

- **low fat cooking spray**
- **1 small onion, chopped finely**
- **1 garlic clove, crushed**
- **200 g (7 oz) canned chopped tomatoes**
- **1 teaspoon tomato purée**
- **2 fresh thyme sprigs, woody stems discarded and leaves chopped**
- **1/2 teaspoon dried oregano or Mediterranean herbs**
- **1 celery stick, sliced finely**
- **1 bay leaf**
- **50 g (1 3/4 oz) thickly sliced lean ham, cubed**
- **200 g (7 oz) canned haricot beans, drained**
- **a small bunch of fresh parsley, chopped**
- **salt and freshly ground black pepper**

- Spray a frying pan with the low fat cooking spray and fry the onion and garlic for 3 minutes, until softened, adding a tablespoon of water, if necessary, to prevent them from sticking.
- Add the tomatoes and tomato purée, thyme, oregano or Mediterranean herbs, celery and bay leaf and bring to the boil. Season and simmer for 5 minutes until thick.
- Add the ham and beans and simmer for a further 5 minutes. Stir through the parsley and then serve.

How to •••

mash potatoes

Using a potato peeler, peel some floury potatoes such as King Edwards. Cut the potatoes into small chunks and put them in a saucepan. Cover with cold water and sprinkle in some salt. Bring the potatoes to the boil, cover and cook for 25 minutes or until they are tender. Remove any scum on the surface of the water, then drain. Add a few tablespoons of skimmed milk and mash together.

 5 POINTS VALUE

Lentil Bolognese

A new way with an **old favourite** that is easy to make, tasty and satisfying.

Ⓥ *20 POINTS values per recipe* takes 20 minutes to prepare, 30 minutes to cook

Serves 4. 478 calories per serving. Freeze ❄ sauce only

- **low fat cooking spray**
- **1 onion, chopped finely**
- **2 garlic cloves, chopped finely**
- **200 g (7 oz) dried red lentils**
- **2 carrots, chopped**
- **1 small butternut squash or 1/4 medium pumpkin, peeled, de-seeded and diced**
- **4 celery sticks, chopped**
- **400 g can chopped tomatoes**
- **2 tablespoons tomato purée**
- **1 teaspoon dried oregano**
- **600 ml (1 pint) vegetable stock**
- **225 g (8 oz) dried spaghetti**
- **salt and freshly ground black pepper**

- Spray a large frying pan with the low fat cooking spray and place on a medium heat. Fry the onion and garlic until softened, about 5 minutes, adding a little water if necessary to stop them from sticking.
- Add the lentils, carrots, squash or pumpkin, celery, tomatoes, tomato purée, oregano and stock. Stir, cover and simmer for 30 minutes. Check the seasoning.
- While the sauce is simmering, cook the spaghetti in plenty of boiling, salted water for 8 minutes or according to the packet instructions, until al dente. Drain and serve with the lentil sauce.

French ham and bean casserole

(3½ POINTS VALUE) Chickpea Chilli

A versatile chilli that can be served as an accompaniment to grilled meat or fish.

ⓨ **14 POINTS values per recipe** takes 15 minutes to prepare, 45 minutes–1 hour to cook

Serves 4. 197 calories per serving. Freeze ✗

- **low fat cooking spray**
- **2 garlic cloves, chopped finely**
- **2 large onions, sliced finely**
- **2 x 400 g cans of chick peas, drained**
- **2 x 400 g cans of chopped tomatoes**
- **1 small red chilli, de-seeded and chopped finely**
- **1 small bunch fresh basil or coriander, chopped, to serve**
- **salt**

● Heat a large non stick frying pan and spray with the low fat cooking spray. Stir fry the onions and garlic for 5 minutes, or until softened, adding a little water if necessary to stop them from sticking.

● Add the chick peas, tomatoes and chilli and bring to a simmer. Simmer gently, stirring every now and then, for 45 minutes to an hour, until reduced and thick. Add salt to taste. Stir in the basil or coriander to serve.

How to ...

slice an onion finely.

If you don't have a food processor but need to chop onions finely, then peel off the skin but don't chop off the roots at the bottom end. Slice the onion in half, then slice it from the top but don't cut into the root as this will hold the onion together. Now slice horizontally across the vertical cuts. Finally, chop off the end roots and discard. Now you should have very finely sliced onions.

(6 POINTS VALUE) Pasta with roasted tomato sauce

ⓨ **24½ POINTS values per recipe** takes 35 minutes to prepare, 45 minutes to cook

Serves 4. 573 calories per serving. Freeze ❄ for up to 1 month

- **24 ripe plum tomatoes, halved**
- **6 garlic cloves, peeled**
- **2 red chillies, de-seeded and chopped**
- **1 tablespoon oregano leaves**
- **low fat cooking spray**
- **2 onions, chopped**
- **500 g (1 lb 2 oz) penne**
- **1 tablespoon basil leaves, torn**
- **salt and freshly ground black pepper**

● Preheat the oven to Gas Mark 3/160°C/fan oven 140°C.

● Place the tomatoes, garlic, red chillies and oregano in a roasting tin and spray with low fat cooking spray. Roast for 45 minutes or until the tomatoes are soft.

● Place the tomato mixture in a food processor and process until the tomatoes are finely chopped.

● Heat a large pan with low fat cooking spray and sauté the onions for 5–6 minutes.

● Cook the pasta in a large pan of boiling salted water for 10 minutes or until al dente.

● Add the tomato mixture, basil leaves and seasoning to the onions and cook for a further 5 minutes.

● Drain the pasta, place in a serving dish and pour over the tomato sauce. Toss gently and serve immediately.

12½ POINTS VALUE ## Lancashire hotpot

A whole meal in just one pot.

49½ POINTS values per recipe takes 25 minutes to prepare, 1½ hours to cook

Serves 4. 529 calories per serving. Freeze ❄ for up to 1 month

- low fat cooking spray
- 8 lamb cutlets, trimmed of fat
- 350 g (12 oz) onions, sliced
- 500 g (1 lb 2 oz) carrots, peeled and sliced
- 900 g (2 lb) potatoes, peeled and sliced
- 4 thyme sprigs
- 2 bay leaves
- 600 ml (1 pint) lamb stock
- 1 tablespoon Worcestershire sauce
- salt and freshly ground black pepper

● Preheat the oven to Gas Mark 4/180°C/fan oven 160°C.

● Heat a frying pan with low fat cooking spray and brown the lamb cutlets for 5–6 minutes on each side. Place four in the base of a deep casserole dish.

● Sprinkle half the sliced onions on top and then layer with half the carrots and half the potatoes. Season each layer and tuck the herbs between them.

● Make another layer of lamb and repeat the layers of vegetables, finishing with potatoes on top.

● Mix together the stock and Worcestershire sauce and pour over the potatoes.

● Cover with a tight fitting lid and cook in the oven for 1 hour. Remove the lid and cook for another 25–30 minutes until the potatoes are browned.

How to ...

cook lamb to perfection.

When cooking meat such as lamb cutlets, adjust the cooking times to suit your taste. This recipe cooks the lamb to medium, but if you like it quite rare, then just cut the cooking time at the end by 15 minutes.

 3 POINTS VALUE ## Braised bacon and summer vegetables

12 POINTS values per recipe takes 25 minutes

Serves 4. 154 calories per serving. Freeze ✗

- low fat cooking spray
- 150 g (5½ oz) bacon steak, fat removed, cut in 1 cm (½ inch) cubes
- 4 garlic cloves, sliced thinly
- 6 spring onions, sliced
- a small bunch of thyme, woody stems removed, leaves chopped
- 225 g (8 oz) broad beans, shelled
- 350 g (12 oz) frozen peas
- 200 ml (7 fl oz) vegetable stock
- grated zest and juice of 1 small lemon
- salt and freshly ground black pepper
- a small bunch of fresh parsley, chopped to garnish

● Heat a large non stick frying pan, spray with the low fat cooking spray and then stir fry the bacon, garlic and spring onions for 5 minutes, or until the onion is softened and the bacon is golden.

● Add the thyme, vegetables, stock and lemon juice. Stir and cook for 5–10 minutes. Then check the seasoning, scatter with the lemon zest and chopped herbs, if using, and serve.

Mushroom frittata

🕐 *1½ POINTS values per recipe* takes 25 minutes

Serves 1. 142 calories per serving. Freeze ✗

low fat cooking spray
1 garlic clove, chopped finely
250 g (9 oz) mushrooms, sliced
1 lemon wedge
1 egg
1 egg white
a few sprigs of parsley or thyme, chopped
salt and freshly ground black pepper

● Heat a small non stick frying pan and spray with the low fat cooking spray, then stir fry the garlic for a minute until golden. With the heat on high add the mushrooms and stir fry for a minute. Season, then squeeze the lemon wedge over them.

● Beat the egg and egg white together with the parsley or thyme in a small bowl until frothy. Then turn down the heat and add to the mushrooms. Cook for 1–2 minutes until the base of the omelette has set.

● Preheat the grill to high, brown the top and then cut into wedges to serve.

 Cajun fish cakes

These spicy fish cakes are typical of the Creole cooking style developed in the southern USA. Serve with a salad of ripe tomatoes, grilled peppers, red onions and fresh basil, dressed with lemon juice.

11 POINTS values per recipe takes 35 minutes

Serves 4. 169 calories per serving. Freeze ✗

300 g (10½ oz) large potatoes, peeled and chopped
1 teaspoon paprika
1 teaspoon cumin seeds
1 teaspoon mustard seeds
1 teaspoon dried oregano
1 teaspoon dried thyme
4 x 150 g (5½ oz) cod fillets
salt and freshly ground black pepper

● Boil the potatoes in a pan of salted, boiling water for 20 minutes, until tender. Drain and mash.

● Meanwhile, grind the spices, herbs and seasoning in a pestle and mortar or spice grinder. Place in a mixing bowl.

● Grill the cod on a foil lined grill pan for about 3 minutes or so on each side, then leave until cool enough to handle. Flake into the bowl of spices, discarding the skin and bones.

● Add the mashed potatoes and mix together. Form into eight patties and grill for 3–4 minutes on each side, until golden brown and crunchy on the top, then serve.

How to ...

separate eggs.

Crack a fresh egg on the side of the bowl and break the egg shell into two halves, using your thumbs to pull it apart. Over a bowl, gently rock the yolk back and forth between the two halves of shell, allowing the white to slip into the bowl. Continue doing this until the white is out, then place the yolk in a separate bowl.

Meals for one

The ethos 'if no one else is there – why does it matter' rings true when you are cooking for yourself. It can be tempting to have a quick, light snack when you have only yourself to think of. Convenience foods and ready meals that are high in fat aren't always the answer either. But if you don't add variety to your meals you may find that you are dissatisfied and bored at mealtimes. Give yourself time to take care of yourself and put a little extra effort into YOU. This chapter will help you discover creativity in your cooking and show you that adding different ingredients, flavours and spices can help to rejuvenate your mealtimes.

Stir fried monkfish with lime (page 102)

[inspiring]

Aubergine Madras

1 POINTS VALUE

A mild curry that makes a satisfying supper for one. Serve with 4 tablespoons of cooked rice for an extra *POINTS* value of 3 per serving. It's also a great accompaniment for grilled meat or fish.

Ⓥ *if using soya yogurt 1 POINTS value per recipe* takes 35 minutes

Serves 1. 91 calories per serving. Freeze ✗

- **1 aubergine, cut in half lengthways**
- **1 teaspoon curry paste**
- **low fat cooking spray**
- **1 small onion, sliced thinly**
- **2 garlic cloves, sliced thinly**
- **1/2 teaspoon ground cumin**
- **1/2 teaspoon ground coriander**
- **1/2 teaspoon garam masala**
- **100 ml (3 1/2 fl oz) vegetable stock**
- **2 tablespoons low fat plain yogurt**
- **2 tablespoons chopped fresh coriander, plus sprigs to garnish**
- **salt and freshly ground black pepper**

● Preheat the oven to Gas Mark 4/180°C/fan oven 160°C. Score the exposed flesh of the aubergine halves with a sharp knife in a deep criss cross fashion and then spread the curry paste over. Place them, cut side up, on a baking tray. Bake for 20 minutes, until softened.

● Meanwhile, spray a non stick frying pan with the low fat cooking spray and stir fry the onion and garlic for 5 minutes, until softened, adding a tablespoon of water, if necessary, to prevent them from sticking. Then add the spices, fry for another minute and turn off the heat.

● When the aubergines are cooked, transfer them to a board and chop them into cubes as marked by the score lines. Add them to the onion mixture, with the stock, and bring to the boil. Boil rapidly, without a lid, for 10 minutes, until the curry is nearly dry.

● Take off the heat, stir in the yogurt, seasoning and coriander and serve.

How to ●●●

make the most of garlic.

Choose plump garlic with white skin and a large stalk. Avoid discoloured garlic as the flavour can be quite rancid. Chopping or crushing garlic releases the flavours. Slice the garlic, or crush it by placing it under the blade of a knife and banging down on the flat of the knife with your hand. Cook garlic with low fat cooking spray to add a lovely flavour.

4½ POINTS VALUE

Rich veggie stew

A dark, thick stew with a delicious tang of fruit and tomato. Serve this stew with some steamed carrots.

Ⓥ *4½ POINTS values per recipe* takes 35 minutes

Serves 1. 345 calories per serving. Freeze ✗

 low fat cooking spray
 1 small onion, chopped
 1 garlic clove, crushed
 100 g (3½ oz) frozen Quorn pieces
 25 g (1 oz) dried apricots, chopped
 15 g (½ oz) sun dried tomato halves, sliced
 200 g (7 oz) canned chopped tomatoes
 200 g (7 oz) floury potatoes, cut in chunks
 salt and freshly ground black pepper

● Heat a non stick saucepan. Spray with the low fat cooking spray. Fry the onion and garlic for about 4 minutes until softened, adding a tablespoon of water, if necessary, to prevent them from sticking.
● Add the Quorn, apricots, sun dried tomatoes, canned tomatoes and 100 ml (3½ fl oz) of water and bring to the boil. Turn down to a simmer and cook for 20 minutes, or until thick and rich, stirring occasionally. Taste and season.
● Meanwhile, boil the potatoes in plenty of salted water for 15–20 minutes or until tender. Drain and serve with the stew.

 6 POINTS VALUE

Fresh tomato and feta pasta

A fresh tasting pasta dish that combines all the flavours of the Mediterranean summer.

Ⓥ *6 POINTS values per recipe* takes 20 minutes

Serves 1. 399 calories per serving. Freeze ✗

 200 g (7 oz) small tomatoes on the vine
 4 garlic cloves, unpeeled
 60 g (2 oz) dried tagliatelle
 2 teaspoons balsamic vinegar
 1 teaspoon olive oil
 ½ teaspoon sugar
 25 g (1 oz) feta cheese, cubed
 a small bunch of fresh basil, torn
 salt and freshly ground black pepper

● Preheat the oven to Gas Mark 7/220°C /fan oven 200°C and place the tomatoes and garlic on a baking tray. Season and roast for 10–15 minutes.
● Meanwhile, cook the pasta in plenty of boiling, salted water for 10–15 minutes, or according to the pack instructions and then drain and return to the saucepan.
● Add the roasted tomatoes, removing and discarding the vine.
● Squeeze the garlic out of the skins and chop the flesh, then add to the pasta with the balsamic vinegar, olive oil, sugar, feta cheese, basil and seasoning. Toss together and serve immediately.

Fresh tomato and feta pasta

Quick curried pork

A very quick curry for one. It is delicious served with egg noodles. A 60 g (2 oz) serving (uncooked weight) of noodles adds an extra **POINTS** value of 3.

3½ POINTS values per recipe takes 15 minutes
Serves 1. 188 calories per serving. Freeze ✗

low fat cooking spray
1 garlic clove, crushed
1 teaspoon Thai red curry paste (see tip)
100 g (3½ oz) lean pork steak, all fat removed, meat sliced finely
2.5 cm (1 inch) piece of fresh root ginger, chopped finely
2 tablespoons stock
1 tablespoon soy sauce
2 tablespoons reduced fat coconut milk
½ teaspoon ground turmeric
juice of ½ lemon
4 pickled garlic cloves, chopped finely

● Heat a large non stick frying pan, spray with the low fat cooking spray and then stir fry the garlic until golden brown. Add the curry paste and stir in.

● Add the pork and stir fry for another 2 minutes until the pork is browned. Then add the remaining ingredients in turn, stirring constantly for a minute or so until heated through.

How to ...

prepare ginger.

Using a sharp knife, cut the length of ginger you need. Carefully slice off the skin with a knife. Holding the ginger at one end slice it very thinly with a sharp knife. Alternatively use a cheese grater to grate the ginger into fine slices.

 ## Steak and ale pie

7 POINTS values per recipe takes 25 minutes to prepare, 50–55 minutes to cook

Serves 1. 403 calories per serving. Freeze ✗

low fat cooking spray
1 small onion, chopped finely
1 carrot, chopped finely
1 celery stick, chopped finely
1 fresh sage sprig, chopped (optional)
100 ml (3½ fl oz) chicken stock
100 g (3½ oz) mushrooms
75 g (2¾ oz) lean sirloin steak, fat removed and meat cubed
1 teaspoon flour
2 tablespoons ale
salt and freshly ground black pepper
For the pastry
50 g (1¾ oz) ready rolled puff pastry
1 teaspoon skimmed milk, to glaze

● Heat a non stick saucepan and spray with the low fat cooking spray. Fry the onion, carrot, celery and sage (if using) for 5 minutes or until softened, adding a little stock if necessary to prevent them from sticking.

● Add the mushrooms, season and stir fry for a further 2 minutes; then remove all the vegetables to a plate.

● Spray the pan again, season and fry the meat until browned all over; then sprinkle with the flour, return the vegetables to the pan and stir it all together.

● Pour over the remaining stock and ale and bring to the boil. Reduce the heat, cover and simmer for 30 minutes on a low heat.

● Meanwhile, roll out the puff pastry to fit an individual pie dish. Preheat the oven to Gas Mark 4/180°C/fan oven 160°C. Spoon the cooked filling into the dish and lay the pastry on top, pressing down at the edges.

● Brush with a little skimmed milk and cut a slit in the middle. Bake for 20–25 minutes or until golden.

Salmon en croûte

Serve this delicious crispy parcel with a big, mixed salad and lemon wedges.

5 POINTS values per recipe takes 20 minutes to prepare, 30 minutes to cook

Serves 1. 430 calories per serving. Freeze ✗

- **2 sheets of 28 x 43 cm (11 x 17 inch) filo pastry**
- **low fat cooking spray**
- **125 g (4¹/₂ oz) skinless, boneless salmon fillet**
- **75 g (2³/₄ oz) frozen, cooked spinach, defrosted and water squeezed out**
- **a pinch of grated nutmeg**
- **1 carrot, grated**
- **a few fresh mint sprigs, chopped**
- **1 small garlic clove, crushed**
- **¹/₂ teaspoon ground turmeric**
- **¹/₂ teaspoon dried chilli flakes**
- **a pinch of ground ginger**
- **salt and freshly ground black pepper**

● Preheat the oven to Gas Mark 4/180°C/fan oven 160°C. Lay the filo sheets on the work surface, one on top of the other, and spray with the low fat cooking spray. Place the salmon in the middle of one end of the stacked filo sheets and season.

● Pile the spinach on the salmon, season again and scatter over the nutmeg.

● Mix all the remaining ingredients together in a bowl and top the spinach with this mixture. Fold the pastry up at the sides and over from the end. Keeping everything in place with the pastry, roll the whole parcel over a few times until the pastry is all used up.

● Place the parcel on a baking tray lined with non stick baking paper. Spray with the low fat cooking spray and then bake for 30 minutes, or until golden brown and cooked right through.

Soy pork with noodles

4¹/₂ POINTS values per recipe takes 30 minutes

Serves 1. 324 calories per serving. Freeze ✗

- **50 g (1³/₄ oz) noodles**
- **low fat cooking spray**
- **1 garlic clove, sliced thinly**
- **1 cm (¹/₂ inch) piece of fresh root ginger, peeled and grated**
- **75 g (2³/₄ oz) lean pork tenderloin, sliced thinly**
- **1 teaspoon light soy sauce**
- **1 tomato, quartered, de-seeded and sliced**
- **¹/₂ celery stick, sliced thinly**
- **1 spring onion, sliced finely**
- **juice of 1 small lime**
- **¹/₂ small green chilli, de-seeded, cored and chopped finely**
- **¹/₂ teaspoon sugar**
- **a handful of fresh coriander, chopped**

● Cook the noodles for 3 minutes in boling water, then drain. Put the noodles in a large bowl and snip them with scissors to make smaller lengths. Spray a non stick frying pan with the low fat cooking spray and fry the garlic and ginger for a few seconds. Add the pork and soy sauce and stir fry for 5 minutes, until the pork is golden.

● Tip everything from the pan over the noodles. Add all the other ingredients, toss together and serve.

How to ...

cut and de-seed chillies.

Wearing rubber gloves, carefully slice the chilli in half vertically. Scrape out the seeds and throw them away. Cut away the white membrane. Slice the chillies very finely and add to the dish. Remove the rubber gloves and wash your hands thoroughly!

Salmon en croûte

Spiced chicken tagine

A warming, sweet and savoury chicken dish – perfect for a winter's evening home alone. Serve this with some steamed zero green vegetables, such as spinach, cabbage or broccoli.

6½ POINTS values per recipe takes 30 minutes

Serves 1. 488 calories per serving. Freeze ✗

- **1 x 150 g (5½ oz) skinless, boneless chicken breast, cut in bite size pieces**
- **1 onion, chopped**
- **½ teaspoon ground ginger**
- **1 small cinnamon stick**
- **½ teaspoon ground coriander**
- **400 ml (14 fl oz) chicken stock**
- **50 g (1¾ oz) no soak prunes, stoned and chopped**
- **5 olives, stoned and chopped**
- **1 teaspoon runny honey**
- **50 g (1¾ oz) couscous**
- **a handful of chopped fresh coriander, to garnish**
- **salt and freshly ground black pepper**

● Put the chicken in a non stick saucepan with the onion, ginger, cinnamon stick, coriander, stock and seasoning. Bring to the boil, cover and simmer, stirring frequently for 15 minutes.

● Add the prunes, olives and honey and cook for a further 5–10 minutes, uncovered, until the sauce is reduced considerably.

● Meanwhile, put the couscous in a bowl and pour over enough boiling water to cover it, with 2.5 cm (1 inch) of boiling water above it. Cover the bowl with a plate, foil or tea towel and leave the couscous to steam for at least 5 minutes. Then fluff up with a fork.

● Check the seasoning in the tagine and remove the cinnamon stick. Serve the chicken accompanied by the couscous and garnished with coriander.

 Chicken with porcini pesto

Serve with lots of green beans or a zero mixed salad, drizzled with balsamic vinegar.

6½ POINTS values per recipe takes 30 minutes

Serves 1. 383 calories per serving. Freeze ✗

- **15 g (½ oz) porcini (dried mushrooms), soaked in hot water for 5 minutes, drained and chopped**
- **15 g (½ oz) pine nut kernels, toasted**
- **1 tablespoon low fat soft cheese with garlic and herbs**
- **1 x 150 g (5½ oz) skinless, boneless chicken breast**

For the sauce
- **low fat cooking spray**
- **1 shallot, sliced**
- **100 g (3½ oz) mushrooms, sliced**
- **½ teaspoon dried oregano or marjoram**
- **1 tablespoon dry white wine**
- **1 tablespoon half fat crème fraîche**
- **salt and freshly ground black pepper**

● Preheat the grill to high. Mix the porcini with the pine nut kernels and soft cheese. Slit the chicken breast on the side to make a pocket. Fill the chicken with the porcini mixture.

● Grill for 4–5 minutes on each side, spooning any filling that comes out on to the top.

● Meanwhile, heat a non stick frying pan and spray with the low fat cooking spray. Fry the shallot until softened.

● With the heat high, add the mushrooms, herbs and seasoning and stir fry for 1 minute. Then add the wine and bubble for a few seconds, incorporating any browned juices from the pan with a wooden spoon.

● Turn down the heat and add the crème fraîche. Stir until hot, but do not allow to boil. Spoon the sauce over the chicken to serve.

(4½ POINTS VALUE) Peperonata with cheesy croûtes

Peperonata is a delicious and warming Italian red pepper stew – great for those chilly autumn days.

4½ *POINTS values per recipe* takes 30 minutes

Serves 1. 376 calories per serving. Freeze ✗

2 red peppers, halved and de-seeded

low fat cooking spray

1 small onion, chopped

2 garlic cloves, sliced thinly

400 g (14 oz) canned chopped tomatoes

1 teaspoon dried oregano

1 teaspoon white wine vinegar

1 teaspoon runny honey

1 tablespoon capers, washed and well squeezed

2 x 2.5 cm (1 inch) thick slices of French bread, sliced diagonally

25 g (1 oz) half fat mature Cheddar cheese, grated

salt and freshly ground black pepper

a handful of chopped fresh parsley, to serve

● Preheat the grill to a high heat and then grill the red peppers, skin side up, for 10 minutes or so, until charred and blistered. Then place in a plastic bag, twist the top to seal and leave until cool enough to handle.

● Meanwhile, heat a large frying pan, spray with the low fat cooking spray. Stir fry the onion and garlic for 5 minutes until softened, adding a couple of tablespoons of water if necessary to prevent them from sticking.

● Add the tomatoes, oregano, vinegar, honey, capers and seasoning and bring to the boil; simmer gently for 15–20 minutes, until the sauce is thick and rich.

● Peel the peppers and slice them. Add to the stew.

● Toast the bread slices on one side under the hot grill. Sprinkle the cheese over the other side and grill for a further 1 minute, until golden and bubbling.

● Spoon the stew on to a plate or serving bowl, scatter over the parsley and eat with the hot cheesy croûtes.

How to ...

skin and peel peppers.

Preheat the grill to high. Slice the peppers in half or quarters. Using a sharp knife, scrape out the seeds and cut away the white fleshy membrane. Place the peppers skin side up and grill them until the skin is blistered and blackened. Carefully remove the peppers, place them in a plastic bag, twist to seal and leave until cool enough to handle. When they are cool, remove the peppers and gently peel away the skin.

(9 POINTS VALUE) Spicy cottage pie

A slight twist on the standard cottage pie. Delicious with steamed or boiled spring greens.

9 POINTS values per recipe takes 30 minutes

Serves 1. 556 calories per serving. Freeze ❄ for up to 1 month

- low fat cooking spray
- 1/2 small onion, diced
- 1 garlic clove, crushed
- 150 g (5 1/2 oz) extra lean beef mince
- 1/2 teaspoon ground cumin
- a pinch of paprika
- 50 ml (2 fl oz) beef stock
- 75 ml (3 fl oz) skimmed milk
- 1/2 tablespoon tomato purée
- 1/2 tablespoon Worcestershire sauce
- 300 g (10 1/2 oz) potatoes, peeled and chopped
- 1 teaspoon wholegrain mustard
- salt and freshly ground black pepper

● Heat the low fat cooking spray in a large pan. Fry the onion for 1–2 minutes and then add the garlic and beef mince.

● Brown the mince all over, then add the spices – stir well and then pour in the beef stock, 50 ml (2 fl oz) of the milk, tomato purée and Worcestershire sauce and seasoning. Simmer for 10–15 minutes, stirring occasionally.

● Meanwhile, boil the potatoes in lightly salted, boiling water until tender and then mash with the remaining milk, wholegrain mustard and seasoning. Preheat the grill.

● When all the cooking liquid has evaporated and you have a rich sauce, spoon the meat into an ovenproof dish. Top with the mashed potatoes and place under a hot grill or at the top of a hot oven for 8–10 minutes until golden and bubbling.

(6 1/2 POINTS VALUE) Szechuan pork

6 1/2 POINTS values per recipe takes 30 minutes to cook

Serves 1. 690 calories per serving. Freeze ✗

- 2 teaspoons Szechuan peppercorns
- 1/4 teaspoon flaked sea salt
- 150 g (5 1/2 oz) pork fillet
- low fat cooking spray
- 60 g (2 oz) wide rice noodles
- 1 pak choi, halved
- 2 teaspoons shredded fresh root ginger
- 2 teaspoons Teriyaki sauce

● Place the peppercorns in a dry frying pan over a medium heat and heat until toasted and fragrant. Place in a pestle and mortar with the salt and crush together.

● Sprinkle the pork with the salt and pepper mixture, patting it into the meat. Heat a frying pan with the low fat cooking spray and cook the pork for 4–5 minutes on each side, or until cooked to your liking. Allow the pork to stand in the pan, off the heat for 5 minutes.

● Cook the wide rice noodles in a pan of boiling water for 4 minutes and then drain.

● Place the pak choi in a steamer (if you don't have a steamer you can use a metal colander over a pan), sprinkle with the ginger and cook for 3–5 minutes, until it is tender.

● Serve the pork, sliced, on top of the pak choi and wide rice noodles. Drizzle with Teriyaki sauce.

Szechuan pork

5½ POINTS VALUE

Colcannon with prawns

Colcannon is a hearty Irish potato dish with cabbage and leeks.

5½ POINTS values per recipe takes 30 minutes

Serves 1. 345 calories per serving. Freeze ✗

- 200 g (7 oz) potatoes, peeled and cubed
- a few leaves of Savoy or other cabbage, shredded
- 75 ml (3 fl oz) skimmed milk
- 1 small leek, chopped
- low fat cooking spray
- 1 garlic clove, chopped
- 100 g (3½ oz) peeled prawns
- juice of ½ lemon
- 1 teaspoon French mustard
- salt and freshly ground black pepper

● Cook the potatoes and cabbage, separately, in boiling salted water for about 15 minutes, or until soft, and then drain.

● Meanwhile, in a small, covered saucepan, heat the milk with the leek for 5 minutes, until the leek is softened.

● Heat the low fat cooking spray in a non stick frying pan and fry the garlic until golden. Add the prawns and stir fry for 1 minute. Pour over the lemon juice and season.

● Mash the potatoes with the leeks and milk, and stir in the drained cabbage, mustard and seasoning. Spoon on to a plate and make a little well in the centre. Fill with the prawns and their juices and serve.

 4½ POINTS VALUE

Blackened salmon on butternut squash

4½ POINTS values per recipe takes 30 minutes to prepare, 45 minutes to cook

Serves 1. 505 calories per serving. Freeze ✗

- 1 medium butternut squash, weighing approx 600 g (1 lb 5 oz)
- 1 teaspoon ground cumin
- 1 salmon fillet, weighing approx 150 g (5½ oz), skinned and any bones removed
- 2 teaspoons soy sauce
- 2 spring onions, sliced on the diagonal into 2.5 cm (1 inch) lengths
- salt and freshly ground black pepper

To serve

- a few sprigs of coriander
- 1 lime wedge

● Preheat the oven to Gas Mark 7/220°C/fan oven 200°C and bake the butternut squash, whole, on a baking tray for 45 minutes, or until soft when pierced with a knife. Peel and mash with seasoning.

● Meanwhile, rub the cumin into the salmon then brush the soy sauce over the fillet.

● When the butternut squash is nearly ready, preheat a non stick griddle pan or the grill until very hot. Griddle or grill the salmon for 3 minutes on one side without moving it, until charred. Turn over with a fish slice and cook the other side for 2–3 minutes, until charred and the fish is just cooked through. Griddle or grill the spring onion alongside for the last few minutes.

● Serve the salmon on a bed of the mashed butternut squash, sprinkled with coriander and served with the lime wedge.

Hungarian goulash

A traditional Hungarian goulash – chunks of beef in a spicy, smooth sauce. Serve with creamy mash or a jacket potato.

5½ POINTS values per recipe takes 25 minutes to prepare, 20–25 minutes to cook

Serves 1. 315 calories per serving. Freeze ❄ for up to 1 month

- **low fat cooking spray**
- **175 g (6 oz) lean fillet steak, cubed**
- **1 small onion, chopped**
- **1 garlic clove, crushed**
- **½ green pepper, de-seeded and sliced**
- **2 teaspoons paprika**
- **100 ml (3½ fl oz) beef stock**
- **½ small can chopped tomatoes**
- **2 teaspoons tomato purée**
- **1 sachet of bouquet garni**
- **50 g (1¾ oz) low fat fromage frais**
- **salt and freshly ground black pepper**

- Preheat the oven to Gas Mark 3/170°C/fan oven 150°C. Heat a pan with the low fat cooking spray and brown the steak for 4–5 minutes. Transfer to a small ovenproof dish.
- Fry the onion in the pan until soft, then add the garlic and green pepper and cook for another minute.
- Stir in the paprika, cook for 1 minute and then pour in the stock, tomatoes, tomato purée and bouquet garni. Bring to the boil for a minute, season and pour over the beef.
- Cook in the oven for 20–25 minutes until the beef is cooked. Remove the bouquet garni, stir in the fromage frais and serve immediately.

Lamb rogan josh

A very spicy dish! Delicious served with 4 tablespoons of cooked rice for an extra *POINTS* value of 3.

4 POINTS values per recipe takes 20 minutes to prepare, 40–50 minutes to cook

Serves 1. 322 calories per serving. Freeze ❄ for up to 1 month

- **1 cm (½ inch) piece of fresh root ginger, peeled and chopped**
- **2 garlic cloves, chopped finely**
- **low fat cooking spray**
- **4 cardamom pods, cracked**
- **1 bay leaf**
- **2 cm (¾ inch) piece of cinnamon stick**
- **175 g (6 oz) cubed shoulder of lamb**
- **1 small onion, peeled and chopped finely**
- **½ teaspoon ground cumin**
- **½ teaspoon ground coriander**
- **¼ teaspoon cayenne pepper**
- **½ teaspoon paprika**
- **1 teaspoon tomato purée**
- **½ teaspoon salt**

- Place the ginger and garlic in a small blender and blend to a paste with 2 teaspoons of water.
- Heat a pan with the low fat cooking spray and add the cardamom pods, bay leaf and cinnamon. Add the lamb pieces and brown all over. Remove the lamb with a slotted spoon.
- Add the onion to the pan. Cook for 3–4 minutes until it begins to brown at the edges. Add the garlic and ginger paste from the blender. Stir for 30 seconds before adding the spices and tomato purée.
- Return the meat to the pan, add the salt and 100 ml (3½ fl oz) water. Stir well and bring to the boil.
- Cover the pan and simmer gently for 40–50 minutes or until the meat is tender.

Bacon wrapped chicken with steamed vegetables

4½ POINTS values per recipe takes 1 hour

Serves 1. 255 calories per serving. Freeze ✗

- **1 lean back bacon rasher**
- **1 chicken breast**
- **½ shallot, diced finely**
- **100 ml (3½ fl oz) chicken stock**
- **1 small carrot, peeled and sliced thinly**
- **25 g (1 oz) mange tout**
- **50 g (1¾ oz) broccoli florets**
- **25 g (1 oz) swede, peeled and chopped**
- **2 teaspoons low fat soft cheese**
- **freshly ground black pepper**

- Preheat the oven to Gas Mark 6/200°C/fan oven 180°C.
- Place the bacon on a chopping board and stretch with the back of a knife. Wrap around the chicken breast. Season with freshly ground black pepper.
- Place the chicken breast in a frying pan over a medium heat, with the shallot, and cook for 5–6 minutes on each side.
- Place the chicken and shallot in a small ovenproof dish and pour over the stock. Cover and cook in the oven for 15–20 minutes.
- Place all the vegetables in a steamer and cook for 10–12 minutes until tender.
- Pour off the chicken stock into a small pan, stir in the soft cheese and bring to a boil for 2–3 minutes to reduce the liquid, keeping the chicken warm.
- Serve the chicken, sliced, on a bed of the vegetables with the reduced sauce poured over the top.

How to ...

steam vegetables

Cut the vegetables into even, bite size chunks and place them in a metal colander. Half fill a saucepan with water and bring to the boil. Place the colander over the boiling water, being careful not to let the colander touch the water. Steam for 10–15 minutes until the vegetables are tender.

 ## Spaghetti carbonara

A fantastically quick and delicious supper. Serve with a zero salad of cherry tomatoes, a few basil leaves, balsamic vinegar and seasoning.

5½ POINTS values per recipe takes 10 minutes

Serves 1. 388 calories per serving. Freeze ✗

- **75 g (2¾ oz) dried spaghetti**
- **2 turkey rashers**
- **50 g (1¾ oz) low fat soft cheese with garlic and herbs**
- **a few fresh basil or parsley sprigs, chopped finely**
- **salt and freshly ground black pepper**

- Cook the spaghetti in plenty of boiling, salted water, for 8–10 minutes, or as instructed on the packet, until just cooked but still a little al dente.
- Meanwhile, grill the turkey rashers as instructed on the pack, until crisp, and then chop into small pieces.
- Drain the pasta and return it to the hot saucepan. Immediately add the soft cheese, seasoning, turkey rashers and basil or parsley. Toss together until the cheese has melted and then serve at once.

(5 POINTS VALUE) Stir fried monkfish with lime

A very satisfying and speedy meal, with the deliciously tangy flavours of lime, garlic and fresh ginger.

5 POINTS values per recipe takes 20 minutes

Serves 1. 495 calories per serving. Freeze ✗

- **low fat cooking spray**
- **1 garlic clove, sliced thinly**
- **2 spring onions, shredded finely**
- **1 cm (1/2 inch) piece of fresh root ginger, sliced into matchsticks**
- **grated zest and juice of 1 lime**
- **2 tablespoons soy sauce**
- **100 g (3 1/2 oz) monkfish tail, central bone removed and flesh sliced thinly**
- **75 g (2 3/4 oz) mange tout, sliced finely**
- **50 g (1 3/4 oz) baby sweetcorn**
- **1 carrot, sliced into fine matchsticks**
- **1/2 red pepper, sliced finely**
- **2 baby courgettes, sliced finely**
- **75 g (2 3/4 oz) dried egg noodles**

● Heat a non stick wok or large frying pan, spray with the low fat cooking spray and then add the garlic, spring onions and ginger. Stir fry over a high heat for 1–2 minutes. Add all the other ingredients except the noodles and cook for a further 3–4 minutes or until the fish is just opaque and cooked through.

● Meanwhile, cook the noodles by putting them in a bowl and covering them with boiling water. Leave to stand for 10 minutes, then drain. Pile the noodles on to a plate and place the fish on top. Serve at once.

How to ●●●

bone monkfish.

Using a sharp knife, slit the fish along the spine from head to tail. Gently pull the flesh back and away from the bone on both sides with a knife. Snip through the spine with scissors and then pull out the spine along with the guts. Discard the spine and guts and rinse the fish well.

 (3 POINTS VALUE) Cook ahead Deep South stew

A rich, warming stew based on the flavours popular in the Southern States of America. Serve with fresh greens such as green beans or broccoli

(Y) *3 POINTS values per recipe* takes 15 minutes to prepare, 15–20 minutes to cook

Serves 1. 253 calories per serving. Freeze ✗

- **low fat cooking spray**
- **1 small onion, sliced finely**
- **1 garlic clove, crushed**
- **50 g (1 3/4 oz) baby carrots**
- **50 g (1 3/4 oz) okra or green beans**
- **50 g (1 3/4 oz) baby sweetcorn**
- **1 tablespoon tomato purée**
- **200 g can of chopped tomatoes**
- **1/2 teaspoon dried chilli flakes**
- **1/2 teaspoon ground cinnamon**
- **200 g can of kidney beans, drained and rinsed**
- **200 ml (7 fl oz) vegetable stock**
- **salt and freshly ground black pepper**

● Spray a large saucepan with the low fat cooking spray and fry the onion and garlic for 5 minutes, adding a little water if they stick, until softened. Add the carrots, okra or green beans, baby sweetcorn, tomato purée, tomatoes, spices, kidney beans, stock and seasoning.

● Bring to the boil and then simmer gently with a lid on for 15–20 minutes or until all the vegetables are tender and the sauce is rich and thick.

Cook ahead Deep South stew

Veggie inspiration

Vegetables are not just for vegetarians. We should all be eating at least five portions of fruit and vegetables a day as part of a healthy lifestyle. But vegetables don't just need to come in piles on the side of your plate – there are many ways in which to add variety and make vegetable dishes more exciting. Experiment with different vegetables as they come into season – you'll be amazed by the different tastes and flavours that they bring to your cooking. Meat-free eating isn't all about vegetables either – there are lots of delicious grains and pulses that can really add interest to your meals. This chapter aims to help you make the most out of your vegetables, add vibrancy to your dishes and make your *POINTS* values go further.

Aubergine cannelloni (page 106)

[delicious]

Aubergine cannelloni

There is no pasta in this 'cannelloni' recipe: slices of grilled aubergine are used to lower the *POINTS* values.

Ⓥ *14¹/₂ POINTS values per recipe* takes 35 minutes to prepare, 35 minutes to cook

Serves 4. 259 calories per serving. Freeze ❄ after step 4

100 g (3¹/₂ oz) long grain rice

2 large aubergines

low fat cooking spray

250 g (9 oz) low fat cottage cheese with onion and chives

a small bunch of fresh parsley, chopped

400 g (14 oz) canned chopped tomatoes with herbs

1 onion, chopped finely

2 garlic cloves, chopped finely

a small bunch of fresh basil, leaves removed and larger ones torn

100 g (3¹/₂ oz) half fat Cheddar cheese, grated

salt and freshly ground black pepper

● Put the rice on to cook as instructed on the packet.

● Meanwhile, preheat the grill to high and slice the aubergines into thin slices lengthways. Season and spray with low fat cooking spray. Grill for 5 minutes on one side, then turn and grill for 2 minutes more, until golden.

● Preheat the oven to Gas Mark 4/180°C/fan oven 160°C. Drain the rice and mix in a large bowl with the cottage cheese, parsley, seasoning and half the tomatoes.

● Spray a non stick frying pan with the low fat cooking spray and fry the onion and garlic for 5 minutes. Add a little water if necessary to prevent them from sticking. Add the rest of the tomatoes and bring to the boil. Simmer for 5 minutes, then season and add the basil.

● Place 2–3 tablespoons of the cottage cheese mixture on each aubergine strip and roll up into a cylinder. Place in one layer in a lasagne dish and pour over the tomato and basil sauce. Scatter with the Cheddar cheese.

● Bake for 35 minutes, until the Cheddar cheese is golden and bubbling. Allow to stand for a few minutes before serving.

 Spring vegetable risotto

A delicious, creamy risotto with low *POINTS* values.

Ⓥ *18¹/₂ POINTS values per recipe* takes 40 minutes

Serves 4. 363 calories per serving. Freeze ✗

225 g (8 oz) baby carrots, trimmed of all but a little of the tender tops

225 g (8 oz) baby turnips, trimmed of all but a little of their tops, quartered

225 g (8 oz) baby courgettes, sliced into thirds diagonally

low fat cooking spray

1 garlic clove, chopped finely

1 onion, chopped finely

300 g (10¹/₂ oz) risotto rice

100 ml (3¹/₂ fl oz) dry white wine

1 litre (1³/₄ pints) boiling hot vegetable stock

a small bunch of fresh parsley, chopped

salt and freshly ground black pepper

20 g (³/₄ oz) Parmesan cheese, to serve

a few parsley sprigs, to garnish

● Steam the spring vegetables for 2–3 minutes, so they are still a little undercooked; then refresh under cold water to stop them from cooking any more.

● Meanwhile, heat a large frying pan and spray with the low fat cooking spray. Stir fry the garlic and onion for 5 minutes, until softened and golden, adding a little water if necessary to prevent them from sticking. Add the rice and mix together.

● Turn the heat to high, pour in the wine and stir fry for a further 2 minutes, until all the wine has been absorbed.

● Turn the heat down to medium, add a ladleful of hot stock, just to cover the rice and cook, stirring, until it is all absorbed. Continue adding one ladleful of stock at a time, following the same method, until all the stock has been absorbed.

● The rice should now be tender but still slightly firm to the bite. Gently fold in the steamed, drained vegetables and parsley. Check the seasoning and serve sprinkled with the Parmesan cheese. Garnish with the parsley sprigs.

Bean and courgette provençal

This is a **quick vegetarian** dish that is great for an al fresco lunch.

Ⓥ *13½ POINTS values per recipe* takes 30 minutes

Serves 4. 176 calories per serving. Freeze ✗

low fat cooking spray

2 large onions, chopped finely

2 garlic cloves, crushed

100 ml (3½ fl oz) dry white wine

225 g (8 oz) cherry tomatoes, halved

2 x 400 g cans of flageolet beans, drained

450 g (1 lb) courgettes, halved lengthways and cut into half moons

10 black olives, stoned and chopped

a small bunch of fresh oregano, chopped, or 2 teaspoons dried oregano

1 tablespoon red wine vinegar

1 tablespoon tomato ketchup

salt and freshly ground black pepper

To serve

1 tablespoon capers

grated zest of 1 lemon

a small bunch of fresh basil, chopped

● Heat a large non stick frying pan and spray with the low fat cooking spray. Then stir fry the onions and garlic for 5 minutes, until starting to brown, adding a little water if necessary to stop them from sticking.

● With the heat up high, add the wine and bubble for a few moments before adding the tomatoes, beans, courgettes, olives, oregano, vinegar, tomato ketchup and seasoning. Cover and cook for 15 minutes.

● Sprinkle with the capers, lemon zest and chopped basil to serve.

Indian sambhar

Ⓥ *14½ POINTS values per recipe* takes 20 minutes to prepare, 15–20 minutes to cook

Serves 4. 292 calories per serving. Freeze ❄

½ teaspoon mustard seeds

½ teaspoon cumin seeds

½ teaspoon dried chilli flakes

6 curry leaves

2 teaspoons dessicated coconut

4 teaspoons vegetable oil

225 g (8 oz) orange lentils, picked, washed and drained

½ teaspoon turmeric

425 ml (¾ pint) vegetable stock

4 tomatoes, chopped

450 g (1 lb) mixed zero vegetables (okra, courgettes, cauliflower, carrots, squash etc), diced

a bunch of fresh coriander, chopped

2 teaspoons vegetable oil

2 garlic cloves, sliced thinly

salt and freshly ground black pepper

● In a medium size non stick saucepan fry the first five ingredients with 2 teaspoons of the oil until the coconut browns. Mix in the lentils, turmeric, stock, tomatoes and seasoning and bring to the boil, then reduce the heat to low.

● Cover and simmer until the lentils are mushy, about 15–20 minutes. Add the vegetables and cook until al dente.

● Meanwhile heat the remaining 2 teaspoons of oil in a small pan and fry the garlic until golden. Pour the garlic over the cooked curry and fold together, then serve.

(6) Wild mushroom risotto

$24\frac{1}{2}$ POINTS value per recipe takes 40 minutes

Serves 4. 418 calories per serving. Freeze ✗

20 g packet of dried mushrooms, e.g. porcini

150 ml (¼ pint) boiling water

low fat cooking spray

1 onion, chopped finely

2 garlic cloves, crushed

350 g (12 oz) risotto rice

100 ml (3½ fl oz) white wine

200 g (7 oz) button mushrooms, sliced

1.2 litres (2 pints) hot vegetable stock

a small bunch of fresh parsley, chopped

salt and freshly ground black pepper

50 g (1¾ oz) Parmesan cheese, grated finely, to serve

- Place the dried mushrooms in a measuring jug and add the boiling water. Soak for 25 minutes.
- Heat a large saucepan, spray with the low fat cooking spray and stir fry the onion and garlic until softened.
- Add the rice and stir to mix well, then add the wine. Drain the dried mushrooms, reserving the water, and chop into small pieces. Strain the soaking water through a fine mesh sieve or piece of muslin and add to the risotto, with the reconstituted and fresh mushrooms.
- Add the stock in small quantities, cooking and stirring frequently until all of it has been absorbed.
- Check the seasoning and stir in the parsley. Serve with the Parmesan cheese sprinkled over the top.

How to ...

cook risotto rice.

Place the risotto rice, such as Arborio, into a saucepan and add just enough water, stock or wine to cover. Simmer until all the liquid is absorbed. Continue adding ladlefuls of stock or water for at least 20 minutes, until all the liquid is absorbed and the rice is al dente.

(4) Grilled Mediterranean quiche

$15\frac{1}{2}$ POINTS values per recipe takes 30 minutes to prepare, 45 minutes to cook

Serves 4. 300 calories per serving. Freeze ✗

low fat cooking spray

2 red peppers

1 aubergine, cut into cubes

2 courgettes, sliced lengthways into 1 cm (½ inch) slices

2 small red onions, cut into wedges

2 tablespoons balsamic vinegar

a small bunch of fresh mint, chopped finely

1 garlic clove, peeled and crushed

2 eggs

150 ml (¼ pint) skimmed milk

1 teaspoon French mustard

salt and freshly ground black pepper

For the pastry

50 g (1¾ oz) polyunsaturated margarine

100 g (3½ oz) plain flour

a pinch of salt

1 egg white, beaten

- Preheat the oven to Gas Mark 7/220°C/fan oven 200°C. Spray a roasting tin with the low fat cooking spray and put the vegetables in. Season, spray with the cooking spray and sprinkle over the vinegar, mint and garlic. Roast for 30 minutes.
- Meanwhile, make the pastry. Rub the margarine into the flour and salt until it resembles fresh breadcrumbs. Add just enough water to bind it into a ball. Wrap in cling film and chill.
- Turn down the oven to Gas Mark 5/190°C/fan oven 170°C. Roll out the pastry and use to line a 19 cm (7½ inch) loose bottomed flan tin. Line with foil and fill with baking beans. Bake for 15 minutes then remove the beans and lining. Bake for a further 10 minutes. Beat the eggs with the milk, seasoning and mustard.
- Spoon the cooked vegetables into the pastry case and pour over the egg mixture. Bake for 20 minutes until set and golden.

Spinach and feta bake

Based on an old Jewish recipe, this is a layered bake with typically Sicilian **sweet and sour** flavours. Serve with a zero green salad dressed with lemon.

19½ **POINTS** *values per recipe* takes 30 minutes to prepare, 35–45 minutes to cook

Serves 4. 348 calories per serving. Freeze ✗

- **750 g (1 lb 10 oz) spinach, washed and tough stems removed, large leaves shredded**
- **2 garlic cloves, crushed**
- **2 tablespsoons capers, rinsed and squeezed to remove excess vinegar**
- **3 medium eggs, lightly beaten**
- **1 tablespoon raisins, chopped finely**
- **50 g (1¾ oz) pine nut kernels, toasted until golden**
- **450 g (1 lb) carrots, peeled and grated**
- **a small bunch parsley, chopped finely**
- **50 g (1¾ oz) ground almonds**
- **50 g (1¾ oz) feta cheese**
- **salt and freshly ground black pepper**

● Put the wet spinach leaves in a pan with a lid over a low heat until they wilt – this should only take a few minutes. Drain and push down into a colander with the back of a large spoon to squeeze out as much of the water as possible.

● Spray a non stick frying pan and fry the garlic for 1 minute then add, with the capers, to the spinach in a bowl and mix together.

● Add two of the eggs, seasoning, raisins and pine nut kernels and tip into a baking dish. Flatten with the back of a large spoon.

● In the same bowl mix the carrots with the remaining egg, parsley and almonds then tip on top of the spinach mixture. Spread out with your fingers then pat down to flatten and compact it.

● Grate over the feta and bake at Gas Mark 4/180°C/fan oven 160°C for 35–45 minutes and then serve.

Red hot pepper pasta

This pasta **dish with a kick** is great as an after work supper or for lunch with friends.

22 **POINTS** *values per recipe* takes 30 minutes

Serves 4. 386 calories per serving. Freeze ✗

- **250 g (9 oz) spinach, tomato or plain dried pasta shapes**
- **200 g (7 oz) watercress, chopped coarsely**
- **100 g (3½ oz) feta cheese, crumbled**
- **1 tablespoon pine nut kernels, toasted**
- **salt and freshly ground black pepper**
- For the sauce
- **4 red peppers, halved and de-seeded**
- **2 garlic cloves, crushed**
- **2 tablespoons balsamic vinegar**
- **1–2 small red chillies, de-seeded and chopped finely**

● Cook the pasta as instructed on the pack, until al dente. Preheat the grill to a high heat.

● Meanwhile, to make the sauce, grill the red peppers skin side up until blistered and blackened. Place in a plastic bag and leave until cool enough to handle.

● Peel off the charred skin and place the flesh in a liquidiser with the other sauce ingredients. Add a few tablespoons or enough water to enable you to process to a smooth purée.

● Drain the pasta and return to the pan. Immediately add the remaining ingredients. Toss, then serve.

Hot and sour noodles

Y *8¹/₂ POINTS values per recipe* takes 30 minutes

Serves 2. 455 calories per serving. Freeze ✗

- 125 g (4¹/₂ oz) rice noodles
- low fat cooking spray
- 1 garlic clove, crushed
- 2.5 cm (1 inch) piece of fresh root ginger, peeled and sliced into matchsticks
- 125 g (4¹/₂ oz) canned bamboo shoots, rinsed and sliced into matchsticks
- 2 carrots, sliced into matchsticks
- 125 g (4¹/₂ oz) beansprouts
- 1 small red cabbage, shredded
- 2 tablespoons soy sauce
- 2 tablespoons plum sauce
- 2 teaspoons sesame oil
- juice of ¹/₂ lime
- 100 g (3¹/₂ oz) radishes, sliced finely
- a small bunch of fresh coriander, chopped

● Cook the noodles as instructed on the packet, or place them in a bowl and cover with boiling water. Leave them to stand for 10 minutes, then drain. Meanwhile, heat a large non stick frying pan or wok, spray with the low fat cooking spray and stir fry the garlic and ginger for a few seconds, until they are golden.

● Add the bamboo shoots and stir fry for a further 5 minutes on a high heat, then add the other vegetables and stir fry for 5 minutes more, until they begin to char on the edges.

● Add the noodles, soy sauce, plum sauce, sesame oil and lime juice. Stir together. Stir in the radishes and coriander and serve.

How to •••

prepare rice noodles.

Put the rice noodles in a bowl. Cover with boiling water or stock. Leave to stand for 10 minutes, gently breaking up the noodles after 5 minutes. Drain the noodles and add to a stir-fry or serve straight away.

 Cashew nut roast

Y *22¹/₂ POINTS values per recipe* takes 50 minutes to prepare + 10 minutes cooling, 1 hour to cook

Serves 4. 380 calories per serving. Freeze ❄

- low fat cooking spray
- 1 onion, chopped finely
- 2 garlic cloves, crushed
- 2 large carrots, grated
- 2 red peppers, grilled, skinned, de-seeded and chopped finely
- 250 g (9 oz) mushrooms, chopped
- 100 g (3¹/₂ oz) fresh breadcrumbs
- 100 g (3¹/₂ oz) cashew nuts, toasted and chopped
- a small bunch of parsley, chopped
- a small bunch of coriander, chopped
- 350 g (12 oz) silken tofu, drained very well and then mashed
- 1 tablespoon Dijon mustard
- 2 tablespoons soy sauce
- salt and freshly ground black pepper
- a few sprigs of parsley, to garnish

For the cranberry sauce

- 250 g (9 oz) frozen cranberries, defrosted
- 2 dessert apples, cored and diced
- 1 tablespoon runny honey

● Make the cranberry sauce by placing all the ingredients for the sauce in a saucepan. Cover, season and bring to the boil. Simmer gently, stirring occasionally, for 15 minutes, until you have a thick sauce.

● Heat a large, non stick frying pan and spray with low fat cooking spray. Fry the onion and garlic until golden.

● Remove from the heat and stir in the rest of the ingredients except the parsley.

● Preheat the oven to Gas Mark 4/180°C/fan oven 160°C. Tip the mixture into a 900 g (2 lb) loaf tin lined with baking paper.

● Bake for 1 hour or until golden brown and firm to the touch. Leave to cool and then serve with the cranberry sauce and parsley.

4½ POINTS VALUE ## Roasted root vegetable pasta

Ⓥ *17 POINTS values per recipe* takes 25 minutes to prepare, 45 minutes–1 hour to cook

Serves 4. 562 calories per serving. Freeze ✗

4 carrots, sliced thickly and diagonally
1 large butternut squash, peeled, de-seeded and sliced into chunks
1 cauliflower, cut and broken into medium florets
4 small turnips, sliced into eighths
1 swede, sliced into wedges
2 garlic bulbs, cut in half horizontally and unpeeled
4 small red onions, sliced into wedges
leaves from 4 rosemary or thyme sprigs, woody stems discarded
4 tablespoons balsamic vinegar plus extra, to serve
2 tablespoons soy sauce
1 teaspoon cumin seeds
low fat cooking spray
350 g (12 oz) pasta, such as pappardelle or fusilli
salt and freshly ground black pepper

● Preheat the oven to Gas Mark 7/220°C/fan oven 200°C. Place all the ingredients except the low fat cooking spray and the pasta in a large, deep baking tray and spread out as much as possible.

● Season all over and spray with the low fat cooking spray. Toss to mix together and then spray again. Roast for 45 minutes–1 hour, until the vegetables are tender and browned at the edges. Toss them around once or twice during the cooking to expose different sides.

● About 15 minutes before the end of roasting time, cook the pasta in plenty of boiling, salted water according to the packet instructions, until al dente. Drain and return to the pan with a few tablespoons of the cooking water.

● Remove the roast vegetables from the oven and squash the garlic out of the baked skins, which should be easy with a wooden spoon; discard the skins. Toss the pasta with the vegetables and garlic. Sprinkle with a few more drops of balsamic vinegar and a light seasoning and then serve.

6 POINTS VALUE ## Courgette and cherry tomato pasta

A very tasty, summery dish, with fresh herbs that add lots of flavour.

Ⓥ *6 POINTS values per recipe* takes 20 minutes

Serves 1. 444 calories per serving. Freeze ❄ for up to 1 month

100 g (3½ oz) tagliatelle
low fat cooking spray
2 spring onions, sliced
1 small courgette, sliced thinly into ribbons with a vegetable peeler
125 g (4 oz) cherry tomatoes, halved
50 g (1¾ oz) low fat fromage frais
½ tablespoon chopped fresh parsley
½ tablespoon chopped fresh mint
½ tablespoon chopped fresh chives
salt and freshly ground black pepper

● Cook the pasta in a large pan of boiling, salted water until al dente.

● Meanwhile, heat the low fat cooking spray in a frying pan. Add the spring onions and courgette ribbons and cook over a medium heat, stirring occasionally, for 3–4 minutes.

● Add the cherry tomatoes and cook for a further 2–3 minutes before stirring in the fromage frais. Season well.

● Drain the pasta and return to the pan.

● Stir the herbs into the courgettes and cherry tomatoes and pour into the pasta. Toss together gently and serve.

How to ●●●
cook pasta.
Place the pasta in a large saucepan. Always be generous with the salt as it brings out the flavour. Add plenty of boiling water, to allow the pasta to swell up and move – otherwise the pasta will become sticky. Cook for 8–10 minutes until the pasta is just tender or al dente.

Piperade

A classic Basque dish with peppers, tomatoes and eggs.

Ⓨ *5 POINTS values per recipe* takes 30 minutes

Serves 2. 258 calories per serving. Freeze ✗

- **1 red pepper, halved and de-seeded**
- **1 green pepper, halved and de-seeded**
- **low fat cooking spray**
- **1 onion, chopped finely**
- **1 garlic clove, crushed**
- **4 ripe tomatoes**
- **4 eggs, beaten lightly**
- **salt and freshly ground black pepper**
- **cayenne pepper or chilli powder, to taste**

● Grill the peppers, skin side up, until charred then pop in a plastic bag and leave until cool enough to handle.

● Meanwhile heat a non stick pan with the low fat cooking spray and fry the onion and garlic until soft, adding a little water if necessary to prevent them from sticking. Peel and dice the peppers.

● Add the tomatoes and peppers to the pan and cook until you have a thick pureé. Lower the heat and stir in the eggs.

● Season and continue stirring until the eggs have cooked to a cream.

How to ●●●

grill and skin peppers.

Cut the pepper in half and de-seed it. Put the peppers on to a baking tray, skin side up and place under a hot grill until the skin chars.

Put the peppers into a plastic bag and leave for 10–15 minutes to allow the steam to get under the skins. When cool, the skins will be easy to peel.

Veggie burgers

Delicious burgers, stuffed full of vegetables and served with a tasty Californian salsa.

Ⓨ *9 POINTS values per recipe* takes 40 minutes

Serves 4. 208 calories per serving. Freeze ✗

- **400 g (14 oz) potatoes, peeled and quartered**
- **500 g (1 lb 2 oz) mixed zero vegetables**
- **low fat cooking spray**
- **2 leeks, chopped roughly**
- **1 garlic clove, chopped**
- **2 tablespoons soy sauce**
- **1 tablespoon tomato purée**
- **1 egg, beaten**
- **a small bunch of fresh parsley, chopped**
- **salt and freshly ground black pepper**

For the salsa
- **100 g (3½ oz) cherry tomatoes, quartered**
- **½ cucumber, diced finely**
- **2 tablespoons tomato juice**
- **1 small red onion, chopped finely**
- **1 teaspoon horseradish sauce**

● Cook the potatoes in salted, boiling water for 15 minutes until tender, then drain. Meanwhile, cook the mixed vegetables in boiling water for 5 minutes and drain.

● Heat a non stick frying pan and spray with the low fat cooking spray. Fry the leeks and garlic for 10 minutes until softened and golden.

● Mash the potatoes, then add the vegetables and other ingredients, including the cooked leeks, garlic and seasoning. Mix well.

● Shape the mixture into eight burgers. Heat a large non stick frying pan and spray with the low fat cooking spray. Fry the burgers for 4–5 minutes on each side.

● Meanwhile, mix all the salsa ingredients together in a bowl. Serve two burgers each with the salsa.

(3) **Garden paella**

 24 POINTS values per recipe takes 20 minutes to prepare, 25 minutes to cook

Serves 8. 257 calories per serving. Freeze ✗

- low fat cooking spray
- 3 garlic cloves, crushed
- 2 red peppers, de-seeded and diced finely
- 450 g (1 lb) ripe tomatoes, chopped
- a generous pinch of saffron strands, soaked in 2 tablespoons boiling water for 5 minutes
- ½ teaspoon paprika or cayenne pepper
- a small bunch of thyme, woody stems removed, leaves chopped
- 400 g (14 oz) long grain or basmati rice
- 1.2 litres (2 pints) vegetable stock
- 2 bay leaves
- 450 g (1 lb) small courgettes, sliced thinly and diagonally
- 225 g (8 oz) peas
- 225 g (8 oz) green beans
- a bunch of spring onions, chopped
- grated zest and juice of 1 lemon
- salt and freshly ground black pepper
- 1 lemon, cut into 8 wedges, to serve

- Heat a large, non stick frying pan or wok and spray with the low fat cooking spray. Stir fry the garlic and peppers for 5 minutes or until golden and softened.
- Add the tomatoes, saffron strands and soaking water, spices, thyme, rice, stock, 100 ml (3½ fl oz) water and bay leaves. Stir together. Cover and cook for 10 minutes.
- Stir the rice and then pile all the remaining vegetables with the lemon juice, zest and seasoning on top. Replace the lid and cook for a further 10 minutes. Uncover and stir.
- Remove the bay leaves, and serve with lemon wedges.

(6½) **Creamy root vegetable curry**

Spicy but not too hot, this curry will become a firm vegetarian favourite.

25 POINTS values per recipe takes 40 minutes

Serves 4. 450 calories per serving. Freeze ✗

- low fat cooking spray
- 1 onion, chopped
- 300 g (10½ oz) swede, peeled and chopped
- 200 g (7 oz) parsnips, peeled and chopped
- 200 g (7 oz) potatoes, chopped
- 2 large carrots, peeled and sliced
- 2 teaspoons curry powder
- 600 ml (1 pint) vegetable stock
- 350 g (12 oz) basmati rice
- 175 g (6 oz) low fat fromage frais
- salt and freshly ground black pepper

- Heat a non stick pan and spray with the low fat cooking spray. Fry the onion for 2–3 minutes.
- Add the remaining vegetables, cover the pan and, over a very low heat, let them sweat for 4–5 minutes.
- Stir in the curry powder and then pour over the stock. Simmer for 15–20 minutes, or until the vegetables are tender.
- Meanwhile, cook the rice in a pan of boiling, salted water for 6–8 minutes until al dente. Drain and keep warm.
- Take out two ladlefuls of vegetables and a little stock. Place these in a food processor with the fromage frais and blend until smooth.
- Return to the pan, stir well and check for seasoning. Serve with the rice.

How to ...

cook perfect rice.

Add 1 part rice to 2 parts cold water. Bring to the boil, then reduce the heat, cover and cook until steam holes appear in the rice. Remove the lid, fluff up the rice with a fork and serve.

Pea and sweet potato curry

A colourful, sweet tasting curry that is also very filling.

Ⓨ **17½ POINTS values per recipe** takes 30 minutes

Serves 4. 287 calories per serving. Freeze ❄ for up to 1 month

- **3 teaspoons cumin seeds**
- **2 teaspoons coriander seeds**
- **2 garlic cloves, chopped**
- **low fat cooking spray**
- **1 large onion, diced**
- **700 g (1 lb 9 oz) sweet potatoes, peeled and chopped**
- **500 ml (18 fl oz) vegetable stock**
- **400 g (14 oz) frozen peas**
- **200 g (7 oz) cottage cheese**

- Dry fry the cumin and coriander seeds to bring out their flavour. Grind in a pestle and mortar with the chopped garlic.
- Heat a pan, spray with the low fat cooking spray and fry the onion for 4–5 minutes until starting to soften.
- Add the sweet potatoes and spice paste. Stir well to coat the potatoes with the spicy mixture.
- Pour in the stock and simmer for 8–10 minutes until the sweet potatoes are nearly cooked.
- Stir in the peas and cottage cheese and heat through for 1–2 minutes.

How to ...

cook sweet potatoes.

Peel the sweet potatoes and cut them into chunks. Cook them in a large pan of boiling water or stock, with a little salt, for 10–12 minutes. Alternatively, spray the chunks with low fat cooking spray and roast at Gas Mark 4/180°C/fan oven 160°C for 20–25 minutes.

 Moroccan vegetable couscous

A traditional dish from Morocco.

Ⓨ **20 POINTS values per recipe** takes 45 minutes

Serves 4. 382 calories per serving. Freeze ✗

- **250 g (9 oz) couscous**
- **425 ml (¾ pint) boiling water**
- **low fat cooking spray**
- **1 garlic clove, crushed**
- **2 red onions, chopped**
- **450 g (1 lb) pumpkin, peeled and cubed**
- **2 carrots, peeled and cubed**
- **400 g (14 oz) canned chopped tomatoes**
- **2.5 cm (1 inch) piece of fresh root ginger, peeled and chopped finely**
- **1 teaspoon ground cinnamon or 1 cinnamon stick**
- **400 g (14 oz) canned chick peas**
- **300 ml (½ pint) vegetable stock**
- **a bunch of fresh parsley or coriander, chopped**
- **salt and freshly ground black pepper**
- **1 large red chilli, de-seeded and chopped finely, to serve (optional)**

- Place the couscous in a large bowl. Pour over the boiling water and allow to stand with a cover on for 15 minutes.
- Meanwhile, heat a wok or large frying pan and spray with the low fat cooking spray. Stir fry the garlic with the onions until they are softened and golden, adding a little water if necessary to prevent them from sticking.
- Add the other vegetables, ginger, cinnamon, chick peas and stock and mix together. Then cover and leave to cook, stirring occasionally, for 15–20 minutes, until the vegetables are softened and the sauce is thick.
- Fluff up the couscous with a fork and then stir into the vegetables. Check the seasoning, and fold in the parsley or coriander. Scatter with the chilli, if using.

Roasted garlic vegetables

Ⓥ *10½ POINTS values per recipe* takes 15 minutes to prepare, 45 minutes to cook

Serves 6. 180 calories per serving. Freeze ✗

low fat cooking spray

2 large aubergines, sliced in half lengthways and then diagonally into thick slices

450 g (1 lb) courgettes, sliced fairly thickly

2 red peppers, de-seeded and cut into 6 lengthways

2 yellow peppers, de-seeded and cut into 6 lengthways

2 garlic bulbs, cut in half crossways and wrapped individually in foil

200 g (7 oz) bulgur wheat

a small bunch of fresh basil, mint or parsley, chopped roughly

2 tablespoons balsamic vinegar

salt and freshly ground black pepper

● Preheat the oven to Gas Mark 7/220°C/fan oven 200°C. Spray two baking trays with low fat cooking spray and spread the aubergines, courgettes and peppers on them. Season and spray again with the low fat cooking spray. Add the garlic parcels and bake for about 25 minutes.

● Meanwhile, cook the bulgur wheat as directed on the packet; then drain and keep aside.

● Place all the roasted vegetables, with the bulgur wheat, herbs and any cooking juices in the baking trays, into a bowl.

● Meanwhile, make the sauce. Unwrap the garlic bulbs and squeeze the pulp out of the skins into a food processor. Add 100 ml (3½ fl oz) of water, the balsamic vinegar and seasoning and blend to a smooth sauce.

● Pour the sauce over the vegetables and bulgur wheat. Toss gently together and then serve.

 Tofu and vegetable kebabs

Use your favourite vegetables to make **colourful kebabs** for a summer barbecue.

Ⓥ *3 POINTS values per recipe* takes 30 minutes + 2 hours marinating

Serves 4. 98 calories per serving. Freeze ✗

50 ml (2 fl oz) soy sauce

1 garlic clove, crushed

2.5 cm (1 inch) piece of fresh root ginger, peeled and chopped

1 teaspoon Tabasco sauce

250 g (9 oz) firm tofu, cut into large cubes

16 cherry tomatoes

1 red pepper, de-seeded and chopped

1 yellow pepper, de-seeded and chopped

1 red onion, cut into 8 chunks

8 large mushrooms, halved

● Mix together the soy sauce, 4½ tablespoons of water, garlic, ginger and Tabasco. Place the tofu in the marinade and leave for at least 2 hours or preferably overnight in the fridge.

● Soak eight wooden kebab skewers in water for 10 minutes to prevent them from burning. Thread the vegetables and tofu on to kebab skewers and cook under a hot grill or over a barbecue for 10–15 minutes, turning regularly, until the vegetables are starting to char at the edges.

How to ● ● ●

make the most of tofu.

Tofu does not have much flavour, but it is a high in protein and vitamin enriched food that absorbs the flavours it is cooked with like a sponge. Always allow enough time to marinate it properly, and use liquid marinades such as soy sauce that will soak into the tofu.

Something special

We all deserve a little luxury in our lives from time to time and this certainly applies to our eating habits. Whether it's a romantic night in for two or a treat for the family, there are bound to be times when a special meal is what's required. But you don't have to opt for the 'blow out' by choosing creamy sauces and lavish desserts. Instead you can choose to take control of the situation. It comes down to understanding what you are eating – and the best way of doing this is to cook it yourself. Don't be afraid to experiment with more exotic ingredients – the more you discover about food, the more variety and interest you will bring to your cooking. This chapter is full of ideas that will help add a little luxury to special occasions, giving you the flexibility to enjoy life without losing sight of your goals.

Fiery king prawn kebabs (page 133)

[luxurious]

Cabbage parcels

Based on the Greek recipe for stuffed vine leaves called dolmathes, this has been adapted to use Savoy cabbage leaves, which have the advantage of being larger to allow more filling.

10 POINTS values per recipe takes 40 minutes to prepare, 35 minutes to cook

Serves 4. 236 calories per serving. Freeze ✗

1 large Savoy cabbage, leaves removed carefully to keep them whole, and then washed

100 ml (3¹/₂ fl oz) white wine

400 g (14 oz) canned chopped tomatoes

1 garlic clove, chopped finely

a small bunch of fresh basil, chopped roughly, to serve

For the stuffing

100 g (3¹/₂ oz) couscous

30 g (1¹/₄ oz) sun dried tomatoes, soaked in boiling water for 5 minutes, then drained and sliced

2 tablespoons pine nut kernels, toasted

8 pieces of porcini, soaked in boiling water for 5 minutes, then drained and chopped

a small bunch of fresh parsley, chopped

a small bunch of fresh mint, chopped

grated zest and juice of 1 lemon

salt and freshly ground black pepper

● Blanch the cabbage leaves in boiling, salted water for 5 seconds; drain and refresh with cold water. Cut large leaves in half by cutting out the middle stem.

● Preheat the oven to Gas Mark 4/180°C/fan oven 160°C. Put the couscous in a bowl and pour over enough boiling water to cover it with 2.5 cm (1 inch) to spare. Cover with a plate, foil or a clean tea towel and leave to steam for 5 minutes. Mix the remaining stuffing ingredients together in the bowl.

● Fill the leaves by placing 1 tablespoon of the stuffing at the stalk end of the leaf and rolling once before folding in the sides and continuing to roll. Secure with cocktail sticks and put in an ovenproof dish. When one layer is complete, season and then start another. (The mixture will make about 20 parcels.)

● Pour over the wine and tomatoes, season, sprinkle over the garlic and cover with foil before baking for 35 minutes. Scatter with the basil and serve.

How to ●●●

prepare couscous.

Place the couscous into a bowl. Pour over just enough hot water or stock to cover the couscous. Cover tightly with a clean tea towel and leave for 15 minutes. This means that no steam escapes – instead it is absorbed into the grain, leaving a lovely fluffy texture. When it is ready, remove the tea towel and fluff up the grains with a fork.

Beef Bourguignon

The long, slow cooking of this wine-rich stew ensures meltingly tender meat. Serve with mashed potato and steamed carrots or broccoli.

15½ POINTS values per recipe takes 25 minutes to prepare, 1½ hours to cook

Serves 4. 207 calories per serving. Freeze ❄

low fat cooking spray

4 rashers lean, back bacon, cut into strips

6 shallots, halved

450 g (1 lb) button mushrooms

2 garlic cloves, peeled and crushed

a small bunch of fresh thyme leaves, chopped

300 g (10½ oz) beef stewing steak, cut into bite size chunks

150 ml (¼ pint) red wine

600 ml (1 pint) chicken stock

1 small can of tomatoes

1 small bunch fresh parsley, chopped, to serve (optional)

salt and freshly ground black pepper

● Preheat the oven to Gas Mark 4/180°C/fan oven 160°C. Heat a large non stick casserole and spray with the low fat cooking spray. Add the bacon, shallots, mushrooms, garlic and thyme and cook gently for 10 minutes adding a little water if necessary to stop them sticking.

● Add the beef and cook for a further 5 minutes. Pour the whole lot into a deep casserole dish, season and add the wine, stock and tomatoes, then cover.

● Bake for 1½ hours, then serve, sprinkled with fresh parsley, if using.

 Rosemary lamb fillets

The delicious smell that fills the house while this dish cooks will have your family or friends queuing up in the kitchen! Serve with minted peas and whole, steamed carrots.

5 POINTS values per recipe takes 30 minutes

Serves 2. 182 calories per serving. Freeze ❄

1 teaspoon ground cumin

8 rosemary sprigs, tough stems removed, leaves chopped finely

1 teaspoon olive oil

2 x 90 g (3 oz) lamb fillets

low fat cooking spray

2 red onions, cut in thin wedges

3 tablespoons balsamic vinegar

salt and freshly ground black pepper

● Mix the cumin, rosemary and seasoning together on a plate. Rub the olive oil into the lamb fillets and roll in the seasoned mixture until covered.

● Heat a frying pan and then gently fry the fillets for 12–15 minutes, turning occasionally, or until cooked through. Remove from the pan to a carving board, cover with foil and leave to rest for a few minutes.

● Meanwhile, spray the pan with the low fat cooking spray and add the onions. Stir fry for 10 minutes, adding a little water if they stick, until softened. Then add the balsamic vinegar and seasoning and stir fry for a further 3–5 minutes. Serve the onions as an accompaniment to the lamb.

Baked marrow gratin

13 POINTS values per recipe takes 40 minutes to prepare, 30 minutes to cook

Serves 4. 230 calories per serving. Freeze ❄ before adding cheese

1 kg (2 lb 4 oz) marrow, halved lengthways and de-seeded

low fat cooking spray

2 onions, chopped finely

2 garlic cloves, crushed

200 g (7 oz) lamb mince

1 teaspoon mixed dried herbs

2 teaspoons Worcestershire sauce

a dash of Tabasco sauce

400 g (14 oz) canned chopped tomatoes

50 g (1¾ oz) dried apricots or prunes, chopped finely

a small bunch of fresh parsley or mint, chopped

50 g (1¾ oz) half fat mature Cheddar cheese

salt and freshly ground black pepper

● Preheat the oven to Gas Mark 6/200°C/fan oven 180°C. Scoop out some of the marrow flesh but leave at least 5 mm (¼ inch) inside the skin to make a firm shell. Chop the flesh finely.

● Heat a large non stick frying pan, spray with the low fat cooking spray and gently fry the onions and garlic for 4 minutes, until softened, adding a little water if necessary to prevent them from sticking.

● Add the mince and break up with a wooden spoon. Season and cook for another 3–4 minutes, until browned all over, then add the chopped marrow and stir together for another minute.

● Add all the other ingredients except the cheese and bring to a simmer. Cover and cook for 10 minutes.

● Place the marrow cases side by side in an oven dish or tray. Pile in the mixture. Add about 150 ml (¼ pint) of cold water to the baking dish, then cover with foil. Bake for 20 minutes.

● Remove the foil, scatter over the cheese and bake for 10 minutes, until the cheese is melted. Divide each case into two.

 Onion and goat's cheese tartlets

These pretty little tartlets make an impressive and tasty dinner party starter.

Ⓥ *8 POINTS values per recipe* takes 35 minutes to prepare, 20–25 minutes to cook

Serves 4. 132 calories per serving. Freeze ✗

low fat cooking spray

450 g (1 lb) onions, sliced thinly

a small bunch of fresh thyme leaves, chopped (optional)

2 sheets of 28 x 43 cm (11 x 17 inch) filo pastry

1 egg

100 ml (3½ fl oz) skimmed milk

1 teaspoon French mustard

50 g (1¾ oz) soft goat's cheese, chopped into small pieces

salt and freshly ground black pepper

● Heat a large, non stick frying pan and spray with the low fat cooking spray. Add the onions, thyme, if using, and seasoning. Stir fry for 2 minutes over a high heat.

● Cover with a piece of baking paper, tucked into the pan, to seal the onions in. Put a lid on the pan and leave to sweat on a low heat for 20 minutes. Check occasionally and stir the onions to make sure they are not sticking to the pan.

● Meanwhile, preheat the oven to Gas Mark 4/180°C/fan oven 160°C. Spray a tray of four individual tart hollows, each about 13 cm (5 inches) in diameter, with the low fat cooking spray. Cut each filo pastry sheet into six equal squares. Lay one square of filo pastry in the bottom of each hollow, with the corners hanging over the sides.

● Repeat with the other pastry sheets until you have three layers in each hollow, with the corners at slightly different angles. Spray with the low fat cooking spray.

● Beat the egg with the milk, mustard and seasoning in a small jug. Spoon the cooked onions into the pastry cases and pour over the egg mixture. Scatter each with an equal portion of the goat's cheese, then bake for 20–25 minutes until set and lightly golden.

Steamed mussels with lemongrass

 ## Braised pheasant with port and mushrooms

A delicious and different way to cook mussels. Serve as a light lunch or supper dish.

11 POINTS values per recipe takes 35 minutes

Serves 4 as a starter or 2 as a main course. 399 calories per serving.

Freeze ✗

- **2 teaspoons vegetable oil**
- **1 onion, chopped**
- **4 garlic cloves, chopped**
- **2 lemongrass stems, chopped**
- **1 small red chilli, de-seeded and chopped (optional)**
- **300 ml (1/2 pint) vegetable stock**
- **1 tablespoon soy sauce**
- **100 ml (3 1/2 fl oz) dry white wine**
- **2 kg (4 lb 8 oz) fresh mussels, cleaned**
- **a small bunch of fresh basil or coriander, chopped roughly**

● Heat the oil in a large saucepan, then add the onion, garlic and lemongrass. Fry gently for a few minutes, then add the chilli (if using), stock, soy sauce and white wine.

● Add the mussels, cover with a lid and cook for 3–4 minutes, shaking occasionally, or until the mussels open (do not overcook or they will become tough).

● Discard any mussels that have not opened. Add the basil or coriander, toss together and then ladle the mussels and all the juices into bowls or soup plates.

This autumnal dish is delicious served with mashed root vegetables such as carrots, swede and turnips or a mixture of these and some meltingly soft braised red cabbage.

17 1/2 POINTS values per recipe takes 35 minutes to prepare + at least 2 hours marinating, preferably overnight, 45 minutes to cook

Serves 4. 292 calories per serving. Freeze ❄

- **400 g (14 oz) pheasant breast fillets, cut into bite size pieces**
- **100 ml (3 1/2 fl oz) port**
- **1 teaspoon dried oregano or Mediterranean herbs**
- **1 large onion, sliced**
- **2 cloves garlic, crushed**
- **450 g (1 lb) chestnut or other mushrooms, cleaned and halved**
- **600 ml (1 pint) chicken stock**
- **salt and freshly ground black pepper**

● Place the pheasant in a shallow bowl and pour over the port and herbs, then leave to marinate for at least 2 hours, but overnight if possible.

● Drain the meat thoroughly, reserving the marinade. In a large non stick pan or casserole, season then dry fry the pheasant until browned all over.

● Add the onion and garlic for 5 minutes, or until softened, then add the mushrooms and season. Add the marinade and scrape up the juices stuck on the bottom of the pan then add the stock and bring to the boil.

● Simmer gently for 35 minutes, covered, then remove the lid and boil rapidly for 10 minutes to reduce the sauce. Check the seasoning and serve.

How to ●●●

prepare mussels.

Discard any open mussels. Scrub the shells with a brush. Remove and discard the beards and then soak the mussels in a sinkful of cold water for at least 10 minutes, before draining and rinsing and draining again.

Fiery king prawn kebabs

2½ POINTS VALUE

The ideal recipe for a romantic dinner for two! Serve with crusty French bread to mop up the juices – a 30 g (1¼ oz) slice of French bread has a **POINTS** value of 1½.

5 POINTS values per recipe takes 20 minutes

Serves 2. 172 calories per serving. Freeze ✗

- 300 g (10½ oz) frozen king prawns without heads (about 12), defrosted
- 3 garlic cloves, sliced thinly
- 2 teaspoons olive oil
- 1 red chilli, de-seeded and chopped finely
- juice of 1 large lemon
- a small bunch of fresh parsley or coriander, chopped
- salt and freshly ground black pepper

● Soak four wooden skewers in water for 10 minutes. Thread the prawns on to the skewers, about three on each, and then lay the skewers on a plate. Preheat the grill or barbecue to high and scatter all the other ingredients over the prawns.

● Reserving the cooking juices, grill or barbecue the prawns for 2–3 minutes on each side, until cooked through and pink. Meanwhile, heat a non stick frying pan and tip in the reserved juices. Fry until sizzling hot.

● Slide the prawns off their skewers with a fork on to two serving plates, then pour over the hot sauce and enjoy.

How to ●●●

make a finger bowl.

Fill a small shallow bowl with warm water and lemon slices. Serve it alongside any seafood dishes in which you use your fingers. Provide napkins to dry your hands.

Smoked salmon pinwheels with roasted asparagus

English Asparagus has a relatively short season, May to June, but it's worth looking out for. Not only does it taste better and cost less than the imported varieties, but it'll be fresher and full of vital nutrients. Roasting asparagus, as opposed to steaming or boiling it, helps to bring out the flavour. Serve it as a stunning starter at a dinner party.

7 POINTS values per recipe takes 10 minutes

Serves 4. 118 calories per serving. Freeze ✗

- **200 g (7 oz) asparagus tips**
- **2 tablespoons balsamic vinegar**
- **200 g (7 oz) thinly sliced smoked salmon**
- **100 g (3¹/₂ oz) low fat soft cheese**
- **1 lemon, cut into wedges, to serve**
- **sea salt and freshly ground black pepper**
- **1 lemon, cut into wedges, to serve**

● Preheat the oven to Gas Mark 6/200°C/fan oven 180°C. Place the asparagus tips in a shallow roasting tray.

● Drizzle over the balsamic vinegar and season, then roast in the oven for 5 minutes until just tender.

● Lay a strip of the smoked salmon on a work surface and spread with a little soft cheese. Place three to four asparagus tips at one end of the strip and roll them up until they are enclosed in the salmon.

● Place on a serving plate and repeat with the other salmon slices and asparagus. Serve scattered with ground black pepper and with lemon wedges to squeeze over.

Provencal trout parcels

This is a recipe from the south of France, which uses a lot of garlic that mellows in flavour as it bakes.

10¹/₂ POINTS values per recipe takes 15 minutes to prepare, 20–25 minutes to cook

Serves 2. 174 calories per serving. Freeze ✗

- **2 shallots, chopped finely**
- **2 medium sized trout, each weighing about 250 g (9 oz), scaled and gutted but heads left on**
- **4 tomatoes, skinned, seeded and chopped**
- **4 garlic cloves, crushed**
- **¹/₄ teaspoon fennel seeds, crushed in a mortar or with a knife**
- **a few sprigs of thyme, woody stems removed**
- **a few sprigs of rosemary, woody stems removed**
- **salt and freshly ground black pepper**
- **a small bunch of fresh parsley, chopped, to garnish**

● Preheat the oven to Gas Mark 4/180°C/fan oven 160°C and prepare two large squares of non stick baking paper big enough to parcel up the fish.

● Place the shallots in the cavities of the fish and then place each fish on a square of paper. Sprinkle over all the other ingredients, except the parsley, and fold up the paper to enclose the fish completely, so that no steam can escape.

● Place the wrapped fish on a baking tray and bake for 20–25 minutes until cooked through.

● Serve the parsley in a small bowl on the table.

How to ...

skin tomatoes.

Bring a pan of water to the boil. Remove from the heat and then dip the tomatoes into the hot water for a minute. Drain the tomatoes and plunge into cold water. You should now be able to slip off the skins with your hands.

Smoked salmon pinwheels with roasted asparagus

Linguine with tomato seafood sauce

15¹/2 POINTS values per recipe takes 30 minutes

Serves 4. 504 calories per serving. Freeze ✗

- **2 x 400 g cans of tomatoes**
- **1 onion, sliced finely**
- **1 teaspoon dried basil**
- **125 g (4¹/2 oz) shrimps or prawns**
- **125 g (4¹/2 oz) scallops**
- **2 garlic cloves, peeled and chopped finely**
- **3 tablespoons chopped fresh parsley**
- **2–3 drops Tabasco sauce, to taste**
- **240 g (8¹/2 oz) linguine**
- **salt and freshly ground black pepper**

- Place the tomatoes, onion, basil and some seasoning in a pan and simmer for 20 minutes, stirring frequently.
- Add the shrimps or prawns, scallops, garlic, parsley and Tabasco sauce. Simmer for 3 minutes.
- Meanwhile cook the pasta in a large pan of boiling, salted water until al dente.
- Drain the pasta and serve with the hot sauce.

Grilled halibut with mango and watermelon salsa

A really fruity salsa to add zing to your fish! Serve this summery dish with 100 g (3¹/2 oz) new potatoes per person for an extra *POINTS* value of 1.

12¹/2 POINTS values per recipe takes 25 minutes

Serves 4. 158 calories per serving. Freeze ✗

- **4 medium halibut steaks**
- **low fat cooking spray**
- **salt and freshly ground black pepper**

For the salsa

- **400 g (14 oz) watermelon, de-seeded and diced**
- **1 mango, stoned, peeled and diced**
- **4 tablespoons freshly chopped chives**
- **1 green pepper, de-seeded and diced**
- **1 red chilli, de-seeded and chopped finely**
- **1 tablespoon lime juice**

- Mix all the salsa ingredients together in a non metallic bowl. Leave to stand at room temperature to enable all the flavours to develop.
- Season the halibut steaks, heat a griddle pan and spray with low fat cooking spray.
- Cook the fish for 4–5 minutes on each side (depending on thickness – try not to over cook as it will become tough).
- Serve the halibut steaks with a couple of spoonfuls of the salsa.

How to •••

prepare scallops.

Buy very fresh scallops. Scrub the closed shells, discarding any 'beard'. Place under the grill for 1 minute to warm them slightly. Holding the scallop, use a sharp knife to push open the shell, lifting off the top. Loosen the scallop and then pull off the grey outer membrane and the fringe. The scallops are now ready to use in cooking.

Grilled halibut with mango and watermelon salsa

(10 POINTS VALUE) Steak with Béarnaise sauce and chips

20 POINTS values per recipe takes 45 minutes

Serves 2. 704 calories per serving. Freeze ✗

700 g (1 lb 9 oz) potatoes, peeled and chopped into chips

low fat cooking spray

sea salt

2 medium lean beef fillet steaks

For the Béarnaise sauce

3 tablespoons white wine vinegar

1 shallot, diced

6 black peppercorns

1 teaspoon dried tarragon

2 egg yolks

1 teaspoon Dijon mustard

150 g (5½ oz) low fat soft cheese

1 tablespoon chopped fresh tarragon

● Preheat the oven to Gas Mark 7/220°C/fan oven 200°C.

● Boil the potatoes in a pan of salted water until just tender. Drain on kitchen paper. Spray a baking sheet with low fat cooking spray and then put the potatoes on it. Spray the chips again and sprinkle with sea salt. Cook in the oven for 15 minutes. Turn them all, then cook for another 10–15 minutes until they are golden.

● Meanwhile, put the vinegar, shallot, peppercorns and dried tarragon into a small pan with 2 tablespoons of water. Bring to the boil and simmer until very little liquid is left. Strain and reserve.

● Put the egg yolks into a bowl over a pan of simmering water. Whisk in the mustard. Gently whisk in the vinegar liquid and finally the soft cheese, a little at a time. If at any stage the sauce starts to look grainy, just pour in a little boiling water and whisk furiously – it will come back together. Stir in the fresh tarragon. Keep warm.

● Grill the steak to your liking and serve with the chips and Béarnaise sauce.

(4 POINTS VALUE) Duck breasts with pepper sauce

This wonderfully rich, creamy sauce goes well with succulent duck breasts – for a special occasion. Serve accompanied by zero vegetables of your choice.

16 POINTS values per recipe takes 25 minutes

Serves 4. 171 calories per serving. Freeze ✗

low fat cooking spray

4 medium, skinless duck breasts (approx 125 g/4 oz each), fat removed

1 red onion, diced

2 tablespoons green peppercorns

100 ml (3½ fl oz) chicken stock

4 tablespoons low fat fromage frais

● Spray a frying pan with the low fat cooking spray and heat. Cook the duck breasts for 5–6 minutes on each side, depending on how rare you like your meat. Remove from the pan and keep warm.

● Add the onion to the pan and cook for 2–3 minutes before adding the remaining ingredients.

● Simmer for 3–4 minutes.

● Slice the duck breasts and serve with the sauce poured over.

How to ●●●

cook duck breast.

Score the flesh and cook in a pan over a high heat. Cook it until it is slightly pink for a really tender, flavoursome meat. Remember to drain off any fat before serving.

(3 POINTS VALUE) Mexican chicken with spicy salsa

An easy, light chicken dish that could be served with a medium baked potato for a *POINTS* value of 2¹/₂ per serving.

6¹/₂ *POINTS values per recipe* takes 20 minutes

Serves 2. 246 calories per serving. Freeze ✗

2 x 150 g (5¹/₂ oz) skinless, boneless chicken breasts

grated zest and juice of 2 limes

¹/₂ teaspoon chilli powder or crushed, dried chilli flakes

¹/₂ teaspoon dried oregano or marjoram

a small bunch of fresh coriander, chopped

low fat cooking spray

salt and freshly ground black pepper

For the salsa

1 mango, skinned and diced

1 small red chilli, de-seeded and chopped finely

¹/₂ small red onion, chopped finely

3 tomatoes, quartered, de-seeded and chopped

● Sprinkle the chicken with the lime zest and juice, chilli, oregano or marjoram, seasoning and half the coriander. Leave to marinate for a few minutes (1 hour would be preferable).

● Meanwhile, mix together all the salsa ingredients with the remaining coriander and seasoning and place in a serving bowl.

● Spray the chicken with the low fat cooking spray. Grill under a hot grill or on a hot griddle for 4–5 minutes on each side until cooked through and golden on the outside. The juices should run clear when pierced with a skewer in the thickest part. Then serve with the salsa.

How to ...

skin and dice a mango.

Slice off the two long sides of the mango as close to the stone as possible. Then cut the flesh into a criss-cross pattern and push the skin inside out so that the cubes of flesh pop up and can be cut out.

(1½ POINTS VALUE) Portabello mushrooms with rice noodles

These not only taste great they also look very impressive for a dinner party.

Ⓥ 6¹/₂ *POINTS values per recipe* takes 40 minutes

Serves 4. 96 calories per serving. Freeze ❄ up to 1 month

8 Portabello mushrooms

200 ml (7 fl oz) vegetable stock

600 ml (1 pint) boiling water

125 g (4¹/₂ oz) very fine stir fry rice noodles

low fat cooking spray

2 cm (³/₄ inch) fresh root ginger, chopped

2 garlic cloves, crushed

2 spring onions, sliced

1 large courgette, grated

1 large carrot, grated

2 tablespoons soy sauce

● Place the mushrooms in a large pan with the stock (you may have to do this in two batches). Bring the stock to the boil, cover the pan and simmer for 5–6 minutes until the mushrooms are cooked. Remove them with a slotted spoon and keep warm.

● Top up the stock with 600 ml (1 pint) boiling water and place the rice noodles in the pan (off the heat). Leave to stand for 4 minutes.

● Meanwhile, heat a frying pan or wok with the low fat cooking spray and stir fry the ginger, garlic and spring onions for 2 minutes. Add the grated courgette and carrot and continue to stir fry for another 2 minutes.

● Stir in the drained noodles and soy sauce and cook for 1 minute.

● Place the mushrooms on a serving plate and, using a spoon and fork, pick up a small amount of the noodles and coil them around the fork. Place the coiled noodles on top of a mushroom. Repeat this on the remaining mushrooms, spooning any juices or vegetables over the noodles. Serve immediately.

Cooking for friends

Entertaining can seem complicated when you are watching your weight, and when we think of dinner parties, healthy wholesome food is not what immediately springs to mind. But you don't need to resort to over-indulgent, rich foods to really impress. The secret is in having the confidence to choose the right combinations of ingredients and flavours to create delicious and satisfying meals. This chapter will help you to enjoy stress-free parties and gatherings.

Mexican tortillas with spicy beef (page 149)

[inviting]

Butterflied tandoori chicken

7 POINTS VALUE

Serve with a vegetable curry such as Aubergine Madras (page 87).

40½ POINTS values per recipe takes 20 minutes to prepare + marinating, 1 hour 20 minutes to cook

Serves 6. 252 calories per serving. Freeze ✗

1.5 kg (3 lb 5 oz) chicken

300 ml (½ pint) low fat plain yogurt

3 garlic cloves, crushed

2.5 cm (1 inch) piece of fresh root ginger, peeled and chopped finely

1 tablespoon tandoori curry paste

1 teaspoon garam masala

salt and freshly ground black pepper

To garnish

2 limes, cut into wedges

a small bunch of fresh coriander, chopped (optional)

● Remove the back bone and ribs from the chicken, turn the chicken so it is skin side up and press down firmly on the breastbone with the heel of your hand to flatten it out.

● Remove all the skin, wash the bird under cold running water and then pat dry with kitchen paper.

● To make the marinade, combine all of the remaining ingredients, except the garnish, in a bowl and then rub all over the chicken both inside and out. Cover and leave it to marinate in the fridge for at least 1 hour and preferably overnight.

● Preheat the oven to Gas Mark 6/200°C/fan oven 180°C and thread two 10 cm (4 inch) metal skewers in a criss-cross fashion through the chicken to keep it flat. Arrange the chicken on a wire rack in a roasting tin spread with some of the marinade and roast for 40 minutes.

● Turn the chicken over, spread with more of the marinade and roast for a further 40 minutes until each side is golden brown and just tender. Leave to rest for a few minutes and then remove the skewers and scatter with the fresh coriander, if using, to serve.

How to •••

remove the back bone and ribs of a chicken.

Use poultry shears or tough kitchen scissors. Cut the chicken along the back and down each side of the back bone. Remove the back bone and discard. Snip the wishbone in half and open out the chicken, then snip out the ribs.

Butterflied tandoori chicken

(3) Shrimp pancakes with garlic prawns

12½ POINTS values per recipe takes 35 minutes + 30 minutes resting

Serves 4. 194 calories per serving. Freeze ✗

low fat cooking spray

6 spring onions, chopped finely, plus extra to garnish

100 g (3½ oz) self raising flour

a large pinch of chilli powder or dried chilli flakes

1 egg

250 ml (9 fl oz) skimmed milk

a small bunch of fresh dill, coriander or parsley, chopped finely

225 g (8 oz) small frozen prawns, defrosted and chopped finely

salt and freshly ground black pepper

For the prawn marinade

16 raw king prawns, heads removed

grated zest and juice of 1 lemon

4 garlic cloves, chopped finely or crushed

● Marinate the king prawns in the lemon zest and juice, along with the garlic and some seasoning.

● Heat a non stick frying pan and spray with the low fat cooking spray, then stir fry the spring onions for 2 minutes, until softened, adding a little water if necessary to prevent them from sticking.

● In a large bowl, combine the flour, chilli and seasoning, then make a well in the middle and add the egg and milk. Gradually stir in until you have a thick batter.

● Stir in the spring onions, herbs and small prawns – the batter should be like thick cream. Leave for 30 minutes.

● Heat a large non stick pan, spray with the low fat cooking spray and drop in tablespoonfuls of the batter. Cook in batches of three or four (the batter should make 12 small pancakes). Cook each batch for a couple of minutes on each side.

● Keep the pancakes warm in a low oven. In the same frying pan or a wok, stir fry the king prawns and the marinade over a high heat for two minutes, until the prawns are cooked through. Serve with the pancakes. Sprinkle with the extra chopped spring onion to garnish.

Shrimp pancakes with garlic prawns

Sweet potato and turkey curry

This curry will warm and cheer you up on a cold winter's evening. Serve with one chapati made without fat, and 1 tablespoon of low fat plain yogurt for an extra **POINTS** value of 2 per serving.

19 POINTS values per recipe takes 45 minutes

Serves 4. 263 calories per serving. Freeze ✗

450 g (1 lb) skinless, boneless turkey breast, cut into bite size pieces

4 sweet potatoes, peeled and cubed

200 ml (7 fl oz) chicken stock

100 g (3½ oz) frozen spinach, defrosted

salt and freshly ground black pepper

a small bunch of fresh coriander, chopped, to garnish

For the marinade

2 teaspoons red or green Thai curry paste

2 tablespoons soy sauce

1 teaspoon sugar

100 ml (3½ fl oz) low fat coconut milk

grated zest and juice of 1 lime

2 fresh red chillies, de-seeded and chopped finely

● In a large bowl, mix together all the marinade ingredients except the lime juice, then add the turkey and stir around until coated. Marinate for at least 30 minutes.

● Meanwhile, cook the sweet potatoes in plenty of boiling, salted water until just tender.

● Remove the turkey from the marinade and stir fry in a non stick wok or frying pan until browned. Add the cooked sweet potatoes, chicken stock, leftover marinade, and spinach.

● Cook for 10 minutes, but do not allow to boil. Stir in the lime juice, season and scatter with the coriander.

 ## Seafood and parsley tart

21½ POINTS values per recipe takes 35 minutes to prepare + 30 minutes chilling, 30–35 minutes to bake

Serves 4. 347 calories per serving. Freeze ✗

For the pastry

50 g (1¾ oz) polyunsaturated margarine

100 g (3½ oz) plain flour, plus extra for dusting

a pinch of salt

1 egg white, beaten

For the filling

low fat cooking spray

4 shallots, chopped

4 garlic cloves, chopped

500 g (1 lb 2 oz) frozen or fresh mixed seafood, defrosted if frozen

50 ml (2 fl oz) dry white wine

a small bunch of fresh parsley, chopped

2 eggs, beaten

150 ml (¼ pint) skimmed milk

salt and freshly ground black pepper

● Make the pastry by rubbing the margarine into the flour and salt until the mixture resembles fresh breadcrumbs. Add 1 tablespoon of cold water and mould into a ball with your hand. Wrap in clingfilm and chill for 30 minutes. Preheat the oven to Gas Mark 6/200°C/fan oven 180°C.

● Roll out the pastry on a floured surface to a circle about 5 mm (¼ inch) thick and use to line a 19 cm (7½ inch) diameter loose bottomed flan tin. Line with foil or baking paper and fill with baking beans. Bake blind for 15 minutes.

● Remove the beans and lining, brush the pastry case with the egg white and bake for 5–10 minutes until golden.

● Lower the oven temperature to Gas Mark 5/190°C/fan oven 170°C and spray a pan with the low fat cooking spray. Fry the shallots and garlic for about 5 minutes until softened, adding a little water if necessary to prevent them from sticking. Then add the seafood, with the white wine and parsley, and heat through.

● In a large bowl, beat the eggs, milk and seasoning. Add the seafood mixture and pour into the pastry case. Bake for 30–35 minutes, until set and lightly browned.

Mexican tortillas with spicy beef

28 POINTS values per recipe takes 50 minutes

Serves 4. 462 calories per serving. Freeze ✗

low fat cooking spray

2 onions, chopped

2 garlic cloves, crushed

300 g (10½ oz) extra lean beef mince

400 g (14 oz) canned chopped tomatoes

½–1 teaspoon dried chilli flakes

1 tablespoon Worcestershire or soy sauce

1/2 teaspoon sugar

100 ml (3½ fl oz) white wine

300 ml (½ pint) vegetable stock

salt and freshly ground black pepper

To serve

8 medium flour tortillas

½ Iceberg lettuce, shredded

For the salsa

6 plum tomatoes, quartered, de-seeded and chopped finely

1 small red onion, chopped finely

1 small red chilli, de-seeded and chopped finely

a small bunch of fresh coriander, chopped

juice of 1 lime

2 teaspoons balsamic vinegar

● Heat a large non stick frying pan, spray with the cooking spray and then stir fry the onions and garlic for 5 minutes, or until softened. Add the beef and stir fry until browned all over. Add the chopped tomatoes, chilli, Worcestershire or soy sauce, sugar, wine, stock and seasoning. Bring to the boil and then simmer for 20 minutes.

● To make the salsa, mix all the salsa ingredients together in a small, non metallic bowl and chill until needed.

● Meanwhile, heat the tortillas as instructed on the packet and then fill with the spicy beef, shredded lettuce and salsa to serve. Alternatively, place all the components in different serving plates and bowls and let diners make their own.

 Porcupine meatballs in red wine sauce

These meatballs, made with rice, are inspired by a New Zealand dish. The rice puffs up as it cooks and sticks out of the meatballs giving them their spiky appearance, hence the name.

23 POINTS values per recipe takes 30 minutes to prepare, 30 minutes to cook

Serves 6. 210 calories per serving. Freeze ✗

low fat cooking spray

1 onion, chopped finely

2 garlic cloves, crushed

400 g (14 oz) extra lean beef mince

150 g (5½ oz) long grain rice

a small bunch of fresh thyme, woody stems removed, leaves chopped, plus extra to garnish

2 carrots, diced finely

100 ml (3½ fl oz) red wine

400 g (14 oz) canned chopped tomatoes

1 tablespoon Worcestershire sauce

300 ml (½ pint) stock

salt and freshly ground black pepper

● Heat a large non stick frying pan, spray with the low fat cooking spray and then stir fry the onion and garlic for 5 minutes, or until softened, adding a little water if necessary to prevent them from sticking.

● Take off the heat and place the onion and garlic in a large bowl with the mince, rice, thyme, carrots and seasoning and mix. Roll into 30 ping pong sized balls, squashing the mixture together with your hands.

● In the same frying pan brown the meatballs on all sides. Add all the remaining ingredients, bring to the boil and then cover and simmer for 30 minutes on a low heat. Serve garnished with the reserved thyme.

5½ POINTS VALUE **Mushroom and spinach filo rolls**

Ⓥ *22½ POINTS values per recipe* takes 35 minutes to prepare, 30 minutes to cook

Serves 4. 388 calories per serving. Freeze ❄ before baking

500 g (1 lb 2 oz) mushrooms, cleaned and chopped finely

100 g (3½ oz) sun dried tomatoes, soaked in boiling water
    for 10 minutes and chopped finely

a small bunch of fresh parsley, chopped finely

2 tablespoons soy sauce

450 g (1 lb) frozen spinach, defrosted and water squeezed out

100 g (3½ oz) low fat soft cheese

½ teaspoon grated nutmeg

400 g pack of frozen filo pastry/16 sheets of 48 x 29 cm
    (18¾ x 11½ inches)

low fat cooking spray

salt and freshly ground black pepper

● Mix the mushrooms, sun dried tomatoes, parsley and soy sauce together in a bowl with some seasoning.

● In another bowl, mix together the spinach with the soft cheese, nutmeg and seasoning.

● Preheat the oven to Gas Mark 4/180°C/fan oven 160°C. Place four sheets of filo pastry on the work surface on top of each other and spray with the low fat cooking spray. Then make a 2.5 cm (1 inch) thick line of spinach going crossways about 5 cm (2 inches) from the top of the top sheet. Also leave about 5 mm (¼ inch) gap at either end to fold the pastry in.

● Then take the mushroom mixture and make another line, of the same thickness, on top of the spinach. Roll up the pastry to make a tube, folding in the ends as you go to seal the roll. Place on a non stick baking tray or non stick parchment on an oven tray.

● Place another four sheets of pastry on the surface, spray and then fill with the two mixtures and roll up as before. Place beside, but not touching, the first roll on the baking tray. Repeat with the third and fourth lots.

● Spray the rolls with the cooking spray and bake for 30 minutes.

 4 POINTS VALUE **Stuffed acorn squash**

Ⓥ *17 POINTS values per recipe* takes 20 minutes to prepare, 50 minutes to cook

Serves 4. 386 calories per serving. Freeze ✗

4 x 300 g (10½ oz) acorn squashes

200 g (7 oz) mixed wild and basmati rice

a small bunch of fresh parsley, chopped finely

1 garlic clove, crushed

4 ripe tomatoes, de-seeded and chopped finely

25 g (1 oz) ready to eat dried apricots, chopped

20 stoned black olives in brine, drained and chopped

50 g (1¾ oz) flaked almonds, toasted until golden

grated zest and juice of 1 lemon

salt and freshly ground black pepper

● Preheat the oven to Gas Mark 5/190°C/fan oven 170°C. Wash the squashes and pierce in several places with the tip of a knife. Bake for 30 minutes, until tender. Leave until cool enough to handle.

● Meanwhile, cook the rice in boiling salted water for 10–15 minutes, until tender, and then drain.

● Slice the lid off the top of each squash, scoop out the seeds and discard. Scoop out some pulp from the centres but leave a thick shell. If the bottom is not flat, cut a thin slice off to make a firm base.

● Roughly chop the pulp and place in a bowl. Add all the other ingredients, including the cooked rice and stir together. Pile back into the squashes and replace the lids on top of the filling.

● Place the squashes in a shallow ovenproof dish and bake for 20 minutes, until golden.

How to ●●●

choose acorn squash.

Look for one that is heavy with smooth, dull skin and no soft spots. Look for orange on the skin as this tells you it's mature and ready to use – too much orange means it is over ripe.

Baked lemon spring chicken

A **fresh tasting**, quick chicken dish. Serve with courgettes and steamed, al dente baby carrots.

14 POINTS values per recipe takes 15 minutes to prepare, 40 minutes to cook

Serves 4. 226 calories per serving. Freeze ✗

- 4 x 165 g (5¾ oz) boneless, skinless chicken breast fillets
- 4 spring onions, chopped finely
- 2 garlic cloves, crushed
- 2 small red chillies, de-seeded and chopped finely (optional)
- grated zest and juice of 2 lemons
- 4 teaspoons olive oil
- salt and freshly ground black pepper

● Preheat the oven to Gas Mark 4/180°C/fan oven 160°C. Put the chicken fillets in a large baking dish lined with foil. Scatter over the remaining ingredients and fold the foil up to enclose the chicken.

● Bake for 40 minutes. Unwrap the foil for the last 10 minutes to allow the chicken to brown.

How to ●●●

keep meat moist.

Wrap the meat or poultry in foil, leaving a section open, and place in a baking tray. Scatter over the meat any marinade ingredients you are using. Wrap up the meat until it is contained in the foil then cook in the oven as required, opening the foil just before the end of cooking to allow the meat to brown. This method seals in the flavour and moisture and does not require any fat for cooking. The same method can be used for fish.

 ## Chicory and blue cheese tart

A **lovely combination** of flavours and textures that makes this an interesting lunch. Serve with a big mixed zero salad.

Ⓥ *14½ POINTS values per recipe* takes 35 minutes to prepare, 40–45 minutes to cook

Serves 4. 211 calories per serving. Freeze ✗

- 15 g (½ oz) polyunsaturated margarine
- 4 heads of chicory, sliced in half lengthways
- 450 g (1 lb) potatoes, peeled and cut in pieces
- 1 teaspoon English mustard
- 50 g (1¾ oz) blue cheese, crumbled
- 1 egg
- 150 ml (¼ pint) skimmed milk
- salt and freshly ground black pepper

● Preheat the oven to Gas Mark 7/220°C/fan oven 200°C. Melt the margarine in a non stick frying pan and gently fry the chicory with a lid on for 20 minutes, until softened.

● Meanwhile, boil the potatoes for about 20 minutes, until cooked. Drain and mash with the mustard and seasoning.

● Line a 20 cm (8 inch) loose bottomed cake tin with non stick baking parchment, pile in the mash and press down to make a base. Bake in the oven for 15 minutes, until it has formed a crust.

● Arrange the braised chicory on top of the potato base and scatter with the blue cheese. In a jug, beat together the egg and milk with some seasoning. Pour over the chicory and return to the oven for a further 10–15 minutes, until the top is golden.

Sweet potato cakes with peppered beef

This is a great way to serve steak – with sweet potato cakes and a piquant mustard dressing.

25½ POINTS values per recipe takes 45 minutes

Serves 4. 386 calories per serving. Freeze ✗

- **700 g (1 lb 9 oz) sweet potatoes, peeled and grated**
- **3 eggs**
- **low fat cooking spray**
- **3 tablespoons cracked black pepper**
- **400 g (14 oz) fillet steak**
- **1 tablespoon wholegrain mustard**
- **3 tablespoons low fat fromage frais**
- **watercress, to serve**
- **salt and freshly ground black pepper**

● Place the grated sweet potatoes in a bowl and mix with the eggs and some seasoning with a fork.

● Heat a frying pan with low fat cooking spray. Add 3 tablespoons of sweet potato mixture and make into flat cakes. Cook for 3 to 4 minutes on each side – until slightly browned – being careful when turning not to break them.

● Cook the remaining sweet potato in the same way. This should make 12 potato cakes. Keep them warm.

● Press the cracked black pepper into the steak and cook in a non stick frying pan for 3–4 minutes on each side or until cooked to your liking. Leave to rest for 2–3 minutes before slicing.

● Mix together the mustard and low fat fromage frais.

● To serve, place three potato cakes on the plate, top with a handful of watercress and the slices of beef. Drizzle with the mustard dressing.

Fragrant lamb curry

This gorgeous curry keeps well in the fridge for a few days or can be made in advance and frozen.

25½ POINTS values per recipe takes 10 minutes to prepare, 1 hour to cook

Serves 4. 208 calories per serving. Freeze ❄

- **low fat cooking spray**
- **350 g (12 oz) lean lamb, cut into bite size pieces**
- **2 large onions, sliced finely**
- **4 garlic cloves, crushed**
- **2 teaspoons curry powder**
- **1 teaspoon garam masala**
- **450 g (1 lb) zero vegetables (such as cauliflower and carrot)**
- **300 ml (½ pint) vegetable stock**
- **150 ml (¼ pint) very low fat plain yogurt**
- **a small bunch of fresh coriander, chopped, to garnish (optional)**
- **salt and freshly ground black pepper**

● Heat a large non stick frying pan and spray with the low fat cooking spray. Season and stir fry the meat for 5 minutes, or until it is browned all over.

● Add the onions and garlic and stir fry for 5 minutes more, adding a little water to prevent them from sticking and to help them soften. Add the curry powder and garam masala and cook for a further 2 minutes.

● Add the vegetables and stock. Bring to the boil then cover and simmer for 15 minutes. Remove the lid and simmer for a further 30 minutes or until the sauce is thick.

● Remove from the heat and allow to cool a little, then stir in the yogurt and fresh coriander, if using, and serve.

Moussaka

34 POINTS values per recipe takes 45 minutes to prepare, 1 hour to cook

Serves 4. 346 calories per serving. Freeze ❄ for up to 1 month

3 aubergines, sliced thickly

low fat cooking spray

2 onions, sliced

2 garlic cloves, chopped

450 g (1 lb) extra lean beef mince

2 tablespoons tomato purée

75 ml (3 fl oz) beef stock

1 teaspoon ground cinnamon

1 tablespoon chopped fresh parsley

3 potatoes, peeled and sliced thickly

3 beefsteak tomatoes, sliced thickly

200 g (7 oz) low fat fromage frais

100 g (3¹/₂ oz) low fat soft cheese

1 egg, beaten

salt and freshly ground black pepper

● Preheat the oven to Gas Mark 6/200°C/fan oven 180°C.

● Place the aubergine slices in a colander. Sprinkle with salt. Place a plate and heavy weight on top. Leave for 30 minutes before rinsing and drying.

● Spray a large pan with low fat cooking spray. Cook the onions and garlic for 4–5 minutes. Add the beef mince. Brown, stirring occasionally.

● Mix together the tomato purée, stock, cinnamon and parsley. Season well. Pour over the beef. Simmer for 15–20 minutes.

● Spray a frying pan with cooking spray and cook the aubergine slices until golden on both sides – you may need to spray more than once. Drain on kitchen paper.

● Place a layer of aubergine slices at the bottom of a casserole dish. Cover with a layer of sliced potatoes and then tomatoes. Spoon over the beef mixture. Continue the layering until you have used everything, finishing with a layer of aubergine.

● Whisk together the low fat fromage frais and soft cheese and then stir in the egg and seasoning. Pour the sauce over the aubergine slices and bake in the oven for 1 hour.

Chicken roasted on garlic and potatoes

A dish for real garlic lovers! Serve with steamed green beans or mange tout.

23 POINTS values per recipe takes 50 minutes

Serves 4. 347 calories per serving. Freeze ✗

> 6 medium potatoes, peeled and chopped
> 100 g (3½ oz) bacon lardons
> 1 tablespoon chopped fresh oregano
> 12 garlic cloves, unpeeled
> low fat cooking spray
> 4 x 165 g (5¾ oz) chicken breasts
> salt and freshly ground black pepper

- Preheat the oven to Gas Mark 6/200°C/fan oven 180°C.
- Place the potatoes, bacon, oregano, garlic and seasoning in a roasting tray. Spray with low fat cooking spray and toss to combine.
- Bake for 15 minutes, toss gently then return to the oven for another 10–15 minutes.
- Meanwhile, season the chicken breasts. Spray a frying pan with low fat cooking spray and cook the chicken for 2–3 minutes on each side until slightly golden.
- Place the chicken on top of the potatoes and garlic and cook for another 10 minutes, until the chicken is cooked through.
- To serve, place the chicken and potatoes on the plates and squeeze the garlic from its skin on top.

 Mediterranean sardines

24½ POINTS values per recipe takes 25 minutes

Serves 4. 334 calories per serving. Freeze ✗

> low fat cooking spray
> 3 garlic cloves, crushed
> 2 shallots, chopped finely
> 1 red chilli, de-seeded and chopped finely
> a small bunch of fresh coriander, chopped
> 8 very fresh sardines, each weighing approx 100 g (3½ oz), cleaned, flattened out and the backbone removed
> 1 lemon, halved
> salt and freshly ground black pepper
> a bunch of fresh herbs such as parsley or coriander, chopped, to serve

- Soak eight cocktail sticks in water for 10 minutes to prevent them from burning under the grill. Heat a non stick frying pan, spray with low fat cooking spray and add the garlic and shallots. Cook for a few minutes with 2 tablespoons of water, then add the chilli, coriander and seasoning.
- Spread this mixture over the flesh side of the sardines, roll them up from head to tail and secure with a cocktail stick. Cook under a hot grill for 3–4 minutes, turning once or twice, until they are cooked through, then squeeze over the lemon and serve.

How to •••

remove the bones from a sardine.

First remove the head then slit along its belly and remove the guts. Lay the sardines on a board, slit side down, skin side up, with the two sides opened out. Gently press down on the backbone through the skin until you feel it give. Do this all along the length of the back and then turn the fish up the other way and gently pull out the backbone. It should come away easily bringing the attached bones with it. Any individual bones that are left can be removed with your fingers. Wash the fish well and it is ready for cooking.

(3 POINTS VALUE) Mushroom and tarragon stuffed chicken

Serve with roasted cherry tomatoes on the vine, seasoned and sprinkled with balsamic vinegar and mashed butternut squash (page 99).

11½ POINTS values per recipe takes 25 minutes to prepare, 30–35 minutes to cook

Serves 4. 196 calories per serving. Freeze ✗

- low fat cooking spray
- 1 small leek, chopped finely
- 1 small courgette, chopped finely
- 1 garlic clove, crushed
- 100 g (3½ oz) mushrooms, chopped finely
- a small bunch of fresh tarragon, woody stems removed, the rest chopped
- 4 x chicken breasts, (150 g/5½ oz each), skinless and boneless
- 2 teaspoons soy sauce
- 150 ml (¼ pint) very low fat plain yogurt
- salt and freshly ground black pepper

● Soak eight cocktail sticks in water for 10 minutes to prevent them from burning. Preheat the oven to Gas Mark 6/200°C/fan oven 180°C. Heat a large non stick frying pan and spray with the low fat cooking spray. Add the leek, courgette, garlic and mushrooms, season and cook for 5 minutes. Remove from the heat and stir in the tarragon.

● Place the chicken breasts between two sheets of baking parchment and beat to an even thickness with a rolling pin. Season, then spread 1 or 2 tablespoons of the tarragon mixture over each breast and roll up, folding in the ends. Secure with cocktail sticks.

● Place the chicken on a non stick baking tray. Bake for 30–35 minutes, until the juices run clear when pierced with a knife. Remove the cocktail sticks. Slice each roll diagonally into three or four pieces.

● To make the sauce, heat the remaining stuffing mixture, then add the soy sauce and yogurt and warm through but do not boil. Check the seasoning and serve with the chicken.

(5½ POINTS VALUE) Stuffed chicken breasts with bacon

A delicious chicken dish stuffed with spinach and garlic.

22½ POINTS values per recipe takes 20 minutes to prepare, 30 minutes to cook

Serves 4. 310 calories per serving. Freeze ✗

- low fat cooking spray
- 4 garlic cloves, chopped finely
- 200 g (7 oz) frozen spinach
- 4 x 150 g (5½ oz) skinless, boneless chicken breasts
- 8 slices of lean back bacon
- 300 ml (½ pint) chicken stock
- salt and freshly ground black pepper

● Heat a non stick frying pan and spray with the low fat cooking spray and then fry the garlic for 2 minutes, until golden. Turn the heat down and add the frozen spinach and cover the pan. After 5 minutes, remove the lid, stir and break up any lumps of spinach and season. Continue to cook gently until the spinach is completely heated through.

● Preheat the oven to Gas Mark 4/180°C/fan oven 160°C. Season the chicken breasts and then slice into the thickest side to make a 'pocket'. Stuff in the spinach. Wrap each breast in two slices of bacon to cover the flesh completely.

● Lay the chicken breasts in a baking tray. Spray with the cooking spray. Pour the stock into the tray and bake for 30 minutes until golden and crisp on the top and cooked through.

● Serve the chicken breasts with the juices from the pan.

How to ●●●

make your own chicken stock.

Place the chicken carcass in a large saucepan with 1 sliced onion, 1 chopped carrot and a few peppercorns. Add 4 litres of water and bring to the boil. Reduce to a simmer and skim off the scum as it rises to the top. Strain the stock and allow it to cool. When cool, remove any congealed fat from the surface. Pour into an ice tray and freeze. Use as required.

Caramelized onion and polenta slice

Polenta is a great dish to serve with stews, meat or ragu sauces.

10 POINTS values per recipe takes 20 minutes to prepare, 50 minutes to cook

Serves 8. 143 calories per serving. Freeze ✗

> **200 g (7 oz) polenta**
> **low fat cooking spray**
> **1 kg (2 lb 4 oz) onions, sliced finely**
> **a small bunch of fresh marjoram, oregano or parsley, chopped**
> **4 large beefsteak tomatoes, sliced**
> **salt and freshly ground black pepper**

● Cook the polenta as instructed on the packet and then pour into a deep 20 cm (8 inch) springform cake tin and allow to cool.

● Heat a large frying pan or wok and then spray with the low fat cooking spray.

● Add the onions and stir fry for a few minutes before turning the heat to low and covering the onions with a sheet of baking parchment and a lid. Cook the onions like this for 30 minutes, until soft and caramelized, stirring occasionally to ensure that they don't burn. Preheat the oven to Gas Mark 4/180°C/fan oven 160°C.

● Sprinkle the herbs, reserving some to garnish, over the polenta, then tip in the onions and spread over. Top with tomatoes and season. Bake for 20 minutes.

● Remove from the tin, scatter with the reserved herbs and cut into eight slices to serve.

How to ...

prepare polenta.

In a pan place one part polenta grain to three parts boiling water. Cover and leave to cook for up to 40 minutes until light and fluffy. Stir occasionally during the cooking to give the grain plenty of air.

  ## Spicy stuffed tomatoes

This Middle Eastern style stuffed tomato dish can be served with a green salad.

7 POINTS values per recipe takes 40 minutes to prepare, 15 minutes to cook

Serves 4. 174 calories per serving. Freeze ✗

> **low fat cooking spray**
> **1 onion, chopped**
> **2 garlic cloves, crushed**
> **450 g (1 lb) potatoes, diced**
> **½ teaspoon turmeric**
> **1 teaspoon garam masala**
> **1 teaspoon ground coriander**
> **1½ teaspoons ground cumin**
> **100 g (3½ oz) frozen peas**
> **a small bunch of fresh coriander, chopped**
> **8 large tomatoes, weighing about 1 kg (2 lb 4 oz)**
> **salt and freshly ground black pepper**
> **2 tablespoons very low fat plain yogurt, to serve**

● Preheat the oven to Gas Mark 6/200°C/fan oven 180°C. Heat a non stick frying pan and spray with the low fat cooking spray. Add the onion and garlic and fry for 2–3 minutes, until softened.

● Add the potatoes and spices and stir fry for 1 minute. Add 300 ml (½ pint) of water, bring to the boil and simmer, covered, for 10 minutes. Remove the lid and simmer for 5 minutes. Add the peas and simmer until the potatoes are cooked. Stir in the coriander and season.

● Slice off the tops and core the tomatoes. Scoop out the insides with a teaspoon or grapefruit knife.

● Put the tomato shells on a baking tray and fill with the potato mixture, then replace the tops. Bake for 15 minutes and serve hot with ½ tablespoon of yogurt each.

 **Prawn and saffron gumbo**

Gumbo is a simple, **thick and tasty** stew from Louisiana. Serve with 4 tablespoons of plain cooked rice for an extra *POINTS* value of 3.

9½ POINTS values per recipe takes 35 minutes

Serves 4. 170 calories per serving. Freeze ✗

- low fat cooking spray
- 3 garlic cloves, crushed
- 3 shallots, chopped finely
- 2 carrots, diced
- ½ teaspoon dried chilli flakes
- 2 teaspoons coriander seeds
- 600 ml (1 pint) chicken or vegetable stock
- 400 g (14 oz) frozen prawns
- 250 g (9 oz) frozen sweetcorn
- 200 g (7 oz) cherry tomatoes, halved
- 200 g (7 oz) okra, green beans or snow peas or mange tout, topped and sliced thinly
- ½ teaspoon ground Cajun spice mix (optional)
- juice of ½ lime
- salt and freshly ground black pepper
- a small bunch of fresh parsley or coriander, chopped, to serve

● Heat a large non stick saucepan and spray with the low fat cooking spray. Fry the garlic and shallots for 5 minutes or so, adding a little water if necessary to prevent them from sticking, until golden and softened.

● Add the carrots, stir fry for a further 5 minutes and then add the chilli flakes, coriander seeds and stock and bring to the boil. Simmer for 5 minutes.

● Add the prawns and sweetcorn, bring back to the boil and then simmer for 5 minutes. Add the tomatoes and green vegetables, simmer for a final 2 minutes and then check the seasoning. Add the Cajun spice mix, if using. Pour over the lime juice, scatter with the herbs and serve.

How to ●●●

make Cajun spice mix.

Combine the following ingredients together in a food processor or pestle and mortar: 2 teaspoons each of salt, cayenne pepper and paprika, 2 bay leaves, 1 teaspoon each of black pepper, dried rosemary and dried chillies and ½ teaspoon each of white pepper, garlic powder, celery salt and ground allspice.

Family food

Meal times with the family should be about enjoying each others company and spending time together. Traditionally, dieting meant cooking a separate meal for yourself, because you didn't want to deprive the rest of the family of the foods that they enjoy. But healthy eating should be something that the whole family can take pleasure in and it can be just as tasty, satisfying and exciting – not to mention the health benefits. Making small positive changes to your cooking methods might be all it takes to change your lifestyle, and the chances are the rest of the family won't even notice. This chapter will help you uncover the little things that make all the difference so that you can make the most of your family meal times.

Roast lamb with mint sauce (page 166)

[relaxing]

Roast lamb with mint sauce

32½ POINTS values per recipe takes 30 minutes to prepare +
15 minutes resting time, 1½–1¾ hours to cook
Serves 8. 220 calories per serving. Freeze ✗

- 2 kg (4 lb 8 oz) leg of lamb
- 6 rosemary sprigs, snipped into smaller sprigs
- 4 garlic cloves, cut in half lengthways
- low fat cooking spray
- 100 ml (3½ fl oz) white wine
- 300 ml (½ pint) vegetable stock
- salt and freshly ground black pepper

For the mint sauce

- a bunch of fresh mint, leaves chopped
- 2 teaspoons caster sugar
- 3 tablespoons cider vinegar
- 4 tablespoons of boiling water

● Preheat the oven to Gas Mark 4/180°C/fan oven 160°C. Put the lamb in a roasting tin and, with a sharp knife, make small slits all over the surface of the lamb joint. Into these slits, push the little sprigs of rosemary and pieces of garlic.
● Season the joint with plenty of salt and pepper, spray with the low fat cooking spray and roast for 1½–1¾ hours.
● Meanwhile, make the mint sauce by mixing together all the ingredients until the sugar has dissolved. Keep in the fridge until you are ready to serve.
● Baste the joint every 30 minutes by spooning over the juices. When the roast is cooked, lift from the roasting tin on to a carving board. Cover with foil and leave for 15 minutes before carving.
● Meanwhile, make the gravy in the roasting tin. Pour the oil out of the tin and discard, then place the tin on the hob and heat. When sizzling, pour in the wine and scrape up all the browned bits from the base of the tin with a wooden spoon and stir well. Add the stock and bring to the boil, still scraping. Allow to bubble for a few minutes. Check the seasoning and strain into a jug.
● Serve three slices (approximately 100 g/3½ oz) per person with the gravy and mint sauce.

Roast pork with apple sauce

This delicious roast can be eaten hot with zero vegetables.

17 POINTS values per recipe takes 25 minutes to prepare, 1¾ hours to cook
Serves 4. 240 calories per serving. Freeze ✗

- 1.5 kg (3 lb 5 oz) boneless shoulder joint of pork
- 4–5 fresh rosemary, thyme or sage sprigs
- salt and freshly ground black pepper

For the apple sauce

- 450 g (1 lb) cooking apples, peeled and chopped
- 2 whole cloves
- 25 g (1 oz) soft brown sugar

For the gravy

- 100 ml (3½ fl oz) Marsala wine or water
- 425 ml (¾ pint) vegetable or chicken stock
- 1 teaspoon Dijon mustard

● Preheat the oven to Gas Mark 4/180°C/fan oven 160°C and rub salt into the skin of the pork. Lay the herbs in a roasting tin and place the joint on top, skin side up. Roast for 1¾ hours.
● Leave to stand on a carving board, covered in foil, for 10 minutes.
● As the roast cooks, make the apple sauce. Put the sauce ingredients in a small saucepan with 4 tablespoons of water and heat gently with a lid on for 10 minutes, until the apple becomes mushy. Remove the cloves to serve.
● As the roast rests, make the gravy. Take the roasting tin, pour off any excess oil and discard, then place the tin on the hob. Heat until the juices start to sizzle, then add the Marsala wine or water and incorporate the juices from the base of the tin as the wine bubbles.
● Add the stock and mustard, then season. Continue to stir, scraping the bottom of the tin to ensure the gravy does not stick. Simmer for 2–3 minutes, then strain into a jug. Serve two slices (approximately 100 g/3½ oz) pork per person.

 **Roast beef with Yorkshire puddings**

A roast is still one of the easiest meals to prepare and cook for family and friends. All the preparation can be done in advance and then you just pop the meat in the oven and enjoy the delicious smells.

33 POINTS values per recipe takes 30 minutes to prepare, 1¾ hours to cook

Serves 6. 200 calories per serving. Freeze ✗

1 kg (2 lb 4 oz) lean roasting joint of beef (sirloin/rib/rump or topside)
2 tablespoons English mustard powder
salt and freshly ground black pepper
For the Yorkshire puddings
1 egg
150 ml (¼ pint) skimmed milk
50 g (1¾ oz) plain flour
low fat cooking spray
For the gravy
100 ml (3½ fl oz) red wine
300 ml (½ pint) beef stock

● Preheat the oven to Gas Mark 4/180°C/fan oven 160°C. Rub seasoning and the mustard powder all over the joint, place in a roasting tray and cover with foil.

● Pour 300 ml (½ pint) of water into the roasting tray and roast for 1¼ hours, for medium cooked meat.

● Meanwhile, make the Yorkshire pudding batter by whisking the egg with the milk and salt in a bowl, then leave for 15 minutes. Add the flour, whisk again until thoroughly mixed and leave until ready to cook.

● Take the beef out of the oven, place on a carving board and cover with foil. Do not wash the roasting tin.

● Turn the oven up again to Gas Mark 7/220°C/fan oven 200°C. Spray a 12 cup non stick patty tin/individual Yorkshire pudding tin with the low fat cooking spray and then place in the oven to heat. After 10 minutes, remove with an oven glove, pour in the prepared batter and return to the oven for 15–20 minutes, until risen and golden.

● Meanwhile, make the gravy in the roasting tin containing the meat juices: using an oven glove, pour any oil out of the tin and discard and then set the tin on the hob over a high heat. Pour over the wine and then the stock, incorporating all the browned juices from the base of the pan with a wooden spoon. Bring to the boil, season and then boil for 1 minute before straining into a serving jug.

● Carve the beef and serve 100 g (3½ oz) per person with the Yorkshire puddings and gravy.

How to ●●●

make gravy.

Once the meat is cooked discard any leftover fat or oil from the roasting tin. Then place the tin on top of the hob. If you like thick gravy, add 1 tablespoon of plain white flour and sir it into the juices. Add 100 ml (3½ fl oz) of wine and 300 ml (½ pint) of stock. Bring to the boil, scraping up any small pieces of meat left in the base of the tin to add flavour. Strain the gravy and serve with the meat.

Toad in the hole with onion gravy

A great family favourite that's so simple to prepare.

19½ POINTS values per recipe takes 30 minutes to prepare, 35–40 minutes to cook

Serves 4. 288 calories per serving. Freeze ✗

- 125 g (4½ oz) plain flour
- 1 egg, beaten
- 300 ml (½ pint) skimmed milk
- low fat cooking spray
- 325 g (11½ oz) low fat sausages
- salt and freshly ground black pepper

For the onion gravy

- low fat cooking spray
- 500 g (1 lb 2 oz) large onions, sliced finely
- 100 ml (3½ fl oz) red or dry white wine
- 300 ml (½ pint) vegetable stock
- a small bunch of fresh thyme, woody stems removed, leaves chopped (optional)

● To make the gravy, heat a large non stick frying pan, spray with the low fat cooking spray and then stir fry the onions for 5 minutes, until they begin to turn golden. Turn the heat to its lowest setting, cover and cook for 20 minutes, stirring occasionally, until softened and coloured.

● Add the wine, stock, thyme, if using, and seasoning. Bring to the boil and then simmer, uncovered, for 10–15 minutes, until thick.

● Meanwhile, to make the toad in the hole, preheat the oven to Gas Mark 6/200°C/fan oven 180°C. Sift the flour into a large bowl and season. Make a well in the middle and then add the egg and half the milk.

● Gradually stir in the flour and whisk until smooth.

● Spray a shallow ovenproof dish with the low fat cooking spray. Arrange the sausages in it. Pour in the batter and bake for 35–40 minutes, until it is well risen.

● Serve the toad cut in sections containing two sausages each, with the onion gravy.

Basque chicken casserole

Most of the cooking for this delicious dish is done in the oven without you having to worry about it.

12 POINTS values per recipe takes 25 minutes to prepare, 1 hour to cook

Serves 4. 265 calories per serving. Freeze ❄

- low fat cooking spray
- 4 x 175 g (6 oz) skinless, boneless chicken breasts
- 225 g (8 oz) shallots, peeled but left whole
- 2 garlic cloves, crushed
- 400 g (14 oz) canned chopped tomatoes
- ½ teaspoon paprika
- 2 red, yellow or orange peppers, de-seeded and chopped
- 2 bay leaves
- 150 ml (¼ pint) dry white wine
- salt and freshly ground black pepper

To serve

- 1 tablespoon capers
- grated zest of 1 lemon
- a small bunch of fresh basil, chopped
- 1 small red chilli, de-seeded and chopped finely (optional)

● Preheat the oven to Gas Mark 2/150°C/fan oven 130°C. Heat a large frying pan and spray with the low fat cooking spray. Season and fry the chicken breasts for 5–6 minutes until golden.

● At the same time, in a large flameproof casserole also on the hob, fry the shallots and garlic with the cooking spray, for 4 minutes, until starting to brown. Add a little water if necessary to prevent them from sticking. Add the tomatoes, and 100 ml (3½ fl oz) of water. Add the paprika, peppers, bay leaves, white wine and seasoning.

● Bring to the boil, incorporate any browned juices from the base of the pan and stir well. Add the browned chicken breasts, cover and cook in the oven for 1 hour.

● Remove from the oven, check the seasoning and sprinkle with the capers, lemon zest, chopped basil and chilli, if using, to serve.

Family fish pie

An easy fish pie that's great for a mid week supper. Serve with your favourite zero vegetables, such as broccoli and carrots.

23 POINTS values per recipe takes 35 minutes to prepare, 20 minutes to cook

Serves 6. 277 calories per serving. Freeze ✗

- 450 g (1 lb) floury potatoes, peeled and cut in chunks
- 450 g (1 lb) pumpkin or butternut squash, peeled and cut in chunks
- 600 ml (1 pint) skimmed milk
- 2 bay leaves
- 500 g (1 lb 2 oz) cod fillets
- low fat cooking spray
- 1 large onion, sliced
- 2 garlic cloves, crushed
- 4 celery sticks or a small fennel bulb, chopped finely
- 150 g (5½ oz) mushrooms, sliced
- 100 g (3½ oz) frozen sweetcorn or peas
- 2 tablespoons cornflour
- a small bunch of fresh parsley
- 1 heaped teaspoon French mustard
- 100 g (3½ oz) half fat mature Cheddar cheese
- salt and freshly ground black pepper

- Boil the potatoes and pumpkin or butternut squash in a saucepan. Cook for 20 minutes, or until tender. Strain but reserve the cooking water. Mash the two together and season.
- Meanwhile, in a large non stick frying pan, heat the milk with the bay leaves and fish fillets until it comes to the boil and then simmer for 1 minute, or until the fish is almost cooked through. Remove the fish to a plate and then strain the milk into a small saucepan and reserve.
- Rinse the frying pan and spray with the low fat cooking spray. Fry the onion and garlic for 5 minutes, until softened, adding 1–2 tablespoons of the reserved potato cooking water if necessary to prevent them from sticking.
- Add the celery or fennel and a few more tablespoons of the potato cooking liquid and cook for a further 5 minutes. Add the mushrooms and cook on a high heat for 3 minutes, until the mushrooms start to give out their juices. Remove from the heat. This mixture needs to be dry, so drain off any juices.
- Break up the fish, removing any skin and bones, and fold into the vegetables with the sweetcorn or peas. Transfer the whole mixture to a large baking dish.
- Preheat the oven to Gas Mark 6/200°C/fan oven 180°C. Take a couple of tablespoons of the reserved milk and mix with the cornflour. Stir this paste back into the rest of the milk and bring to the boil, stirring, until it thickens; then add the parsley, mustard and seasoning.
- Pour the parsley sauce over the fish mixture and fold gently together. Top with the potato and squash mash. Scatter over the grated cheese and bake for 20 minutes, until the cheese is golden and bubbling.

How to •••

skin fish.

Lay the fish fillet skin side down and make a small cut at the tail end, through the flesh to the skin. Place the fish with the tail towards you, then put the blade of the knife under the skin where it has been cut. Holding the skin firmly with your other hand slide the blade away from you, up to the head of the fish, then discard the skin.

Winter casserole with herb dumplings

POINTS VALUE 6

A delicious, warming and filling casserole – perfect on a cold and frosty winter's day.

23¹/2 POINTS values per recipe takes 35 minutes to prepare, 15–20 minutes to cook

Serves 4. 390 calories per serving. Freeze ✗

300 g (10¹/2 oz) parsnips, chopped into 1 cm (¹/2 inch) dice

2 teaspoons olive oil

low fat cooking spray

8 shallots, cut in half lengthways

2 garlic cloves, sliced finely

350 g (12 oz) carrots, sliced thinly diagonally

350 g (12 oz) turnips, cut into 2.5 cm (1 inch) chunks

1 tablespoon cornflour

200 ml (7 fl oz) cider

200 g (7 oz) button mushrooms, cleaned

350 ml (12 fl oz) vegetable stock

1 bay leaf

salt and freshly ground black pepper

For the dumplings

125 g (4¹/2 oz) self raising flour

50 g (1³/4 oz) half fat Cheddar cheese, grated

a small bunch of fresh parsley, chopped finely

50 g (1³/4 oz) polyunsaturated margarine

- Preheat the oven to its highest setting and toss the parsnips with the olive oil and seasoning. Roast for 20–25 minutes, until golden brown; keep warm.
- Meanwhile, heat a large non stick saucepan and spray with the low fat cooking spray. Add the shallots and garlic and fry for 4 minutes until softened, adding a little water if necessary to prevent them from sticking.
- Add the carrots and turnips and stir fry a further 5 minutes. Mix the cornflour in a small bowl with 2 tablespoons of the cider. Add the mushrooms, stock, remaining cider and bay leaf to the pan. Cover and cook for 5 minutes.
- Meanwhile, make the dumplings by mixing the ingredients, together with seasoning, but reserving a little chopped parsley. Add about 1 tablespoon of water to make a soft dough. Form into about 16 walnut size balls and set aside.
- Add the cornflour paste and seasoning to the stew and bring back to the boil, stirring occasionally. Once thickened, add the dumplings carefully so that they are about three quarters immersed. Cover and simmer for 15–20 minutes, until the dumplings have risen.
- Scatter the parsnips over the top, with the reserved chopped parsley, and serve.

How to ...

make dumplings.

Mix together 125 g (4¹/2 oz) self raising flour, 50 g (1³/4 oz) half fat Cheddar cheese, some herbs, seasoning and 50 g (1³/4 oz) margarine. Rub together until combined and crumbly and then add a little water until you have a soft dough. Split the dough and roll into small balls. Add the dumplings to a casserole dish for about 15–20 minutes before the end of cooking. Cook until the dumplings are risen and golden.

Cod in parsley sauce

This classic British sauce goes well with any fish. Serve each portion with 100 g (3½ oz) minted new potatoes and 2 heaped tablespoons of peas for an extra *POINTS* value of 2 per serving. Mange tout and sweetcorn are also delicious on the side.

18 POINTS values per recipe takes 40 minutes

Serves 4. 280 calories per serving. Freeze ✗

600 ml (1 pint) skimmed milk

1 large bunch of parsley, leaves separated from stalks, chopped finely

2 tablespoons polyunsaturated margarine

4 tablespoons plain flour

1 teaspoon Dijon or wholegrain mustard

low fat cooking spray

4 x 150 g (5½ oz) cod fillets, skinned

salt and freshly ground black pepper

4 lemon wedges, to serve

● Heat the milk with the parsley stalks until it's nearly boiling, then strain. Melt the margarine on a low heat in a medium non stick saucepan. Add the flour to the margarine and stir until it becomes a ball of thick paste.

● Add the milk a bit at a time and, after each addition, stir vigorously until you have a thick, smooth paste. Keep adding the milk, stirring until the sauce is smooth and thick. If it looks lumpy at any point, just stop adding milk and continue to heat and stir vigorously until it is smooth again.

● Stir the chopped parsley into the milk sauce, with the mustard and seasoning. Turn off the heat.

● Preheat the grill to a medium setting. Set the cod fillets on the grill pan on a piece of foil sprayed with the low fat cooking spray. Season the fillets and grill for 5–6 minutes until just cooked through, turning once and seasoning again.

● Put the fillets on to serving plates. Serve with the parsley sauce poured over and lemon wedges.

7 POINTS VALUE Lamb chops with bashed neeps

A deliciously simple recipe that can be on the table in half an hour. Serve with fresh, zero steamed greens such as broccoli, beans or spinach. 'Neeps' is the Scottish word for turnips.

28 POINTS values per recipe takes 30 minutes

Serves 4. 373 calories per serving. Freeze ✗

8 x 60 g (2¼ oz) lamb chops

low fat cooking spray

2 garlic cloves, crushed

150 ml (¼ pint) orange juice

4 tablespoons redcurrant jelly

150 ml (¼ pint) vegetable stock

1 tablespoon cornflour

For the bashed neeps

450 g (1 lb) turnips, peeled and chopped

450 g (1 lb) carrots, peeled and chopped

150 ml (¼ pint) very low fat fromage frais

salt and freshly ground black pepper

● To make the bashed neeps, put the turnips and carrots on to cook in plenty of boiling, salted water for 20 minutes or so, until very tender. Drain and, when cooled a little, mash together with the fromage frais and seasoning.

● Meanwhile, preheat the grill. Place the chops on a grill pan and season. Spray a small non stick saucepan with the low fat cooking spray. Fry the garlic for a minute or so, until golden. Add the orange juice, redcurrant jelly and stock. Heat, stirring, until the jelly has dissolved. Mix the cornflour with 2 tablespoons of water to make a paste, then add to the other ingredients in the pan. Bring the sauce to the boil, stirring until it thickens. Season to serve with the chops and neeps.

● Meanwhile grill the chops for 3–4 minutes on each side until golden, seasoning when you turn them.

● Serve the chops with the bashed neeps and sauce.

3 POINTS VALUE Fish goujons with tartare sauce

Serve these crisp coated fish pieces as finger food, with the creamy tartare sauce as a dip.

17½ POINTS values per recipe takes 35 minutes

Serves 6. 201 calories per serving. Freeze ✗

100 g (3½ oz) plaice, skinned and cut in thick strips

50 g (1¾ oz) plain flour, seasoned with ½ teaspoon chilli powder and salt

2 large egg whites, beaten

300 g (10½ oz) fresh breadcrumbs

lemon wedges, to serve

For the tartare sauce

100 g (3½ oz) low fat soft cheese

200 ml (7 fl oz) very low fat plain fromage frais

2 tablespoons capers, rinsed and squeezed to remove excess vinegar

4 small gherkins, chopped finely

2 spring onions, chopped finely

a small bunch of fresh dill or fennel, chopped

salt and freshly ground black pepper

● Preheat the grill to a medium heat. Dip some of the fish strips first in the chilli flour, then in the egg whites and finally in breadcrumbs. Spread out on a grill pan lined with foil.

● Grill the goujons until golden and crisp and cooked through, turning over once or twice to brown all over. Repeat with the remaining fish strips.

● Meanwhile, make the tartare sauce by beating together the soft cheese and fromage frais and then stirring in all the other ingredients with some seasoning. Tip into a serving bowl and serve with the goujons, with the lemon wedges to squeeze over.

4½ POINTS VALUE **Cheesy pasta bake**

A really creamy, cheesy pasta dish with sugar snap peas for crunch.

18½ **POINTS values per recipe** takes 35 minutes to prepare, 15–20 minutes to cook

Serves 4. 322 calories per serving. Freeze ❄ for up to 1 month

225 g (8 oz) rigatoni pasta

low fat cooking spray

1 red onion, diced

75 g (2¾ oz) baby button mushrooms, quartered

75 g (2¾ oz) sugar snap peas, halved lengthways

125 g (4½ oz) baby spinach leaves

150 g (5½ oz) low fat soft cheese

1 tablespoon shredded basil leaves

6 plum tomatoes, sliced

175 g (6 oz) cottage cheese

salt and freshly ground black pepper

- Preheat the oven to Gas Mark 4/180°C/fan oven 160°C.
- Bring a pan of salted water to the boil and cook the pasta for 8 minutes or until al dente.
- Meanwhile, heat a pan with low fat cooking spray and cook the onion for 2–3 minutes before adding the mushrooms and sugar snap peas. Cook for 3–4 minutes, stirring occasionally.
- Drain the pasta and return to the pan with the spinach. Stir around gently to wilt the spinach.
- Stir in the mushroom and sugar snap peas mixture along with the soft cheese. Stir well to mix, then add seasoning.
- Pour the pasta into an ovenproof dish and top with the tomato slices. Spoon over the cottage cheese and bake in the oven for 15–20 minutes.

5 POINTS VALUE **Lasagne**

30 **POINTS values per recipe** takes 40 minutes to prepare, 30–35 minutes to cook

Serves 6. 250 calories per serving. Freeze ❄ for up to 1 month

low fat cooking spray

1 small onion, chopped finely

2 unsmoked bacon rashers, chopped finely

1 garlic clove, crushed

200 g (7 oz) extra lean beef mince

1 teaspoon dried basil

400 g can of chopped tomatoes

2 tablespoons tomato purée

150 ml (¼ pint) beef stock

200 g (7 oz) low fat fromage frais

50 ml (2 fl oz) soya milk

50 g (1¾ oz) low fat soft cheese

a pinch of nutmeg

225 g (8 oz) lasagne sheets

salt and freshly ground black pepper

- Preheat the oven to Gas Mark 4/180°C/fan oven 160°C.
- Heat a frying pan with the low fat cooking spray and cook the onion, bacon and garlic for 5 minutes.
- Add the beef and brown, stirring constantly.
- Stir in the basil, chopped tomatoes, tomato purée, beef stock and seasoning. Bring to a simmer. Cover and cook for 15–20 minutes.
- Mix together the fromage frais, soya milk and soft cheese to make a smooth white sauce. Add the nutmeg and seasoning.
- Spread about a quarter of the beef sauce over the base of an ovenproof dish. Cover with sheets of lasagne and a few spoonfuls of white sauce. Repeat these layers, finishing with a final layer of white sauce. Bake in the oven for 30–35 minutes until the sauce is bubbling and golden.

(5 POINTS VALUE) Salmon and dill fish pie

A tomato based fish pie with sweet, fresh dill and succulent salmon. Serve with a crisp green salad.

21 POINTS values per recipe takes 20 minutes

Serves 4. 324 calories per serving. Freeze ❄ filling for up to 1 month

- **750 g (1 lb 10 oz) potatoes, peeled and chopped**
- **325 g (11½ oz) salmon fillet**
- **150 ml (5 fl oz) skimmed milk**
- **low fat cooking spray**
- **175 g (6 oz) mushrooms, chopped**
- **2 celery sticks, diced**
- **100 g (3½ oz) fresh spinach**
- **6 tablespoons low fat fromage frais**
- **3 tablespoons chopped fresh dill**
- **salt and freshly ground black pepper**

- Preheat the oven to Gas Mark 6/200°C/fan oven 180°C.
- Boil the potatoes in a pan of salted boiling water until tender.
- Place the salmon and milk in a small pan and simmer for 4–5 minutes until the salmon is just cooked. Drain, reserving the milk. Flake the salmon into big chunks.
- Heat a pan with low fat cooking spray and add the mushrooms and celery and cook for 4–5 minutes. Stir in the spinach, cover the pan and cook for another 2–3 minutes until the spinach has wilted.
- Add the salmon and fromage frais, stir well to combine and simmer for 1–2 minutes before stirring in the freshly chopped dill and seasoning. Pour into a shallow dish.
- Drain the potatoes and mash with 100 ml (3½ fl oz) of the milk that was used to cook the salmon. Season well and spoon over the salmon.
- Place in the oven and cook for 10 minutes until the potato topping is bubbling and golden.

 ## (3 POINTS VALUE) Turkey and vegetable casserole

A lovely, warming winter dish, ideal for feeding the whole family.

12½ POINTS values per recipe takes 25 minutes to prepare, 40–50 minutes to cook

Serves 4. 274 calories per serving. Freeze ✗

- **low fat cooking spray**
- **1 large onion, sliced**
- **450 g (1 lb) turkey breast meat, cut into bite size pieces**
- **1 fennel bulb, sliced**
- **2 carrots, peeled and sliced**
- **1 leek, sliced**
- **350 g (12 oz) butternut squash, peeled and sliced**
- **450 g (1 lb) potatoes, peeled and sliced**
- **600 ml (1 pint) chicken stock**
- **1 tablespoon Worcestershire sauce**
- **salt and freshly ground black pepper**

- Preheat the oven to Gas Mark 6/200°C/fan oven 180°C.
- Heat a frying pan with low fat cooking spray and cook the onion for 4–5 minutes. Remove from the pan and place in a deep casserole dish.
- In the same pan, cook the turkey meat until browned on all sides. Place this in the casserole dish on top of the onion.
- Layer the remaining vegetables over the turkey, ending with a layer of potatoes on the top.
- Mix together the stock and Worcestershire sauce and pour over the casserole. Season well, cover with a lid and cook for 40–50 minutes.

How to ...

add an aniseed flavour to food.

Strip fennel leaves and add to dressings or sauces. Alternatively add the bulb to soups, stews or casseroles during cooking to add a subtle aniseed flavour to the dish.

Roast chicken with lemon and thyme

36½ POINTS values per recipe takes 40 minutes to prepare, 1¼ hours to cook

Serves 6. 180 calories per serving. Freeze ✗

1 medium chicken, weighing approx 1.5 kg (3 lb 5 oz)

low fat cooking spray

3 lemons, cut into chunky wedges

2 garlic cloves, crushed

a small bunch of fresh thyme, woody stems removed, chopped

300 ml (½ pint) chicken stock

salt and freshly ground black pepper

● Preheat the oven to Gas Mark 6/200°C/fan oven 180°C. Place the chicken in a roasting tray and spray with low fat cooking spray. Season and squeeze the juice from the wedges of one lemon over the skin and then place the squeezed lemon shells inside the cavity.

● Slide your fingers under the skin of the chicken and smear the crushed garlic with a little of the thyme over the breast meat.

● Roast for about 30 minutes, basting frequently with the juices in the tray. Remove from the oven and surround the bird with the remaining lemon wedges and sprinkle with the thyme. Spray with low fat cooking spray, season and baste with any juices from the chicken, then return to the oven for another 45 minutes, until the chicken is cooked through.

● To test if the chicken is cooked, stick a skewer or knife into the meatiest portion of one of the thighs. The juices that run out should be clear rather than bloody.

● When cooked, remove the chicken to a carving board, cover with foil and keep warm while you make the gravy.

● To make gravy, drain off any excess oil in the tin then place the tin on the hob. Heat until the juices boil, then add the stock.

● Scrape up any juices stuck to the tin with a wooden spoon or spatula and boil rapidly for a few minutes until the gravy is reduced a little. Strain the gravy into a jug and serve with the carved meat, garnished with the remaining thyme and the roasted lemon wedges.

Turkey and mushroom potato topped pie

22½ POINTS values per recipe takes 55 minutes

Serves 4. 396 calories per serving. Freeze ✗

low fat cooking spray

1 large onion, chopped

2 lean back bacon rashers, sliced

500 g (1 lb 2 oz) turkey breast meat, cut into bite size pieces

275 g (9½ oz) mushrooms, sliced thickly

300 ml (½ pint) chicken stock

5 or 6 sprigs fresh thyme

900 g (2 lb) potatoes, peeled and chopped

2 leeks, sliced

100 g (3½ oz) low fat fromage frais

3 tablespoons skimmed milk

salt and freshly ground black pepper

● Preheat the oven to Gas Mark 6/200°C/fan oven 180°C. Heat a large pan with low fat cooking spray and cook the onion and bacon for 3–4 minutes. Add the turkey and cook for 5–6 minutes before adding the mushrooms, stock, thyme and seasoning. Simmer for 15 minutes.

● Meanwhile cook the potatoes in a pan of boiling, salted water until tender and fry the leeks in a frying pan with low fat cooking spray.

● When the turkey is cooked, stir in the low fat fromage frais and, using a slotted spoon, spoon the mixture into an ovenproof dish. Pour in half of the liquid discarding the rest.

● Mash the potatoes with the skimmed milk and then using a fork, stir in the leeks. Season well.

● Top the turkey mixture with the potatoes and leeks and place in the oven for 15 minutes.

Quorn shepherds pie

17 POINTS values per recipe takes 50 minutes

Serves 4. 373 calories per serving. Freeze ❄

- **750g (1 lb 10 oz) potatoes, peeled and diced**
- **4 parsnips, peeled and diced**
- **low fat cooking spray**
- **2 carrots, peeled and diced finely**
- **2 celery sticks, diced finely**
- **2 onions, chopped finely**
- **2 garlic cloves, peeled and crushed**
- **300 g (10½ oz) Quorn mince**
- **600 ml (1 pint) vegetable stock**
- **400 g can of chopped tomatoes**
- **a dash of Tabasco sauce**
- **4 tablespoons skimmed milk or soya milk**
- **50 g (1¾ oz) frozen peas**
- **salt and freshly ground black pepper**

- Cook the potatoes and parsnips in a large pan of boiling, salted water for 10–15 minutes until tender.
- Meanwhile, heat a large frying pan and spray with the low fat cooking spray.
- Stir fry the carrots, celery, onions and garlic for 5 minutes, until softened, adding a little water if necessary to prevent them from sticking.
- Add the Quorn and stock, bring to the boil and simmer rapidly for 10 minutes. Add the tomatoes and Tabasco sauce and simmer a further 10 minutes until thick. Check the seasoning.
- Preheat the grill to high, drain the potatoes and mash with the seasoning.
- Spoon the Quorn mixture into an ovenproof dish. Top with the mash and then grill for 2 minutes until bubbling and golden.

Pork goulash with tagliatelle

27 POINTS values per recipe takes 30 minutes to prepare, 20 minutes to cook

Serves 4. 527 calories per serving. Freeze ❄ goulash only

- **low fat cooking spray**
- **450 g (1 lb) onions, chopped**
- **2 garlic cloves, crushed**
- **2 red peppers, de-seeded and chopped**
- **400 g (14 oz) lean pork steaks, any fat removed, cut in bite size pieces**
- **200 g (7 oz) mushrooms, halved**
- **600 ml (1 pint) tomato juice**
- **½ teaspoon paprika**
- **a few thyme or rosemary sprigs, tough stems removed, leaves chopped**
- **350 g (12 oz) dried tagliatelle**
- **salt and freshly ground black pepper**

- Heat a large non stick saucepan or casserole dish, spray with the low fat cooking spray. Add the onions, garlic and peppers. Cook for 15 minutes, stirring occasionally, or until the vegetables are softened, adding a little water if necessary to prevent them from sticking.
- Meanwhile, heat a large non stick frying pan and spray with the low fat cooking spray. Season the pork and fry over a high heat until browned all over. Add the mushrooms and stir fry for a further 2–4 minutes.
- Add the pork and mushrooms to the casserole or saucepan, together with the tomato juice, paprika and herbs. Bring to the boil and then simmer, covered, for 20 minutes, until the sauce is reduced and the pork is tender.
- 15 minutes before the end of cooking, cook the tagliatelle in boiling, salted water until tender. Drain the tagliatelle and serve topped with goulash.

6½ POINTS VALUE **Garlic roast pork with mash**

Creamy, garlicky mash topped with garlic pork chops.

25½ POINTS values per recipe takes 20 minutes to prepare, 50 minutes to cook

Serves 4. 366 calories per serving. Freeze ✗

- **450 g (1 lb) pork loin**
- **2 garlic bulbs, unpeeled**
- **4 garlic cloves, chopped**
- **600 g (1 lb 5 oz) potatoes, peeled and chopped**
- **125 ml (4 fl oz) skimmed milk**
- **200 g (7 oz) broccoli, cut into florets**
- **salt and freshly ground black pepper**

- Preheat the oven to Gas Mark 7/220°C/fan oven 200°C.
- Make slits between the pork flesh and the bones and place the meat in a baking dish with the garlic bulbs.
- Sprinkle the chopped garlic into the slits in the meat and rub the joint with seasoning. Roast for 25 minutes until golden.
- Remove the garlic bulbs and reduce the oven temperature to Gas Mark 4/180°C/fan oven 160°C. Cook the pork for another 25–35 minutes.
- Meanwhile, cook the potatoes in a pan of boiling salted water until they are tender. Drain and add the skimmed milk. Squeeze out the cooked garlic from the bulbs and mash together until creamy.
- Serve the pork, sliced into thick pieces on a bed of garlicky mash with steamed or boiled broccoli.

 4 POINTS VALUE **Chilli con carne**

33 POINTS values per recipe takes 30 minutes to prepare, 1½ hours to cook

Serves 8. 260 calories per serving. Freeze ❄

- **low fat cooking spray**
- **2 large onions, chopped finely**
- **4 garlic cloves, crushed**
- **600 g (1 lb 5 oz) extra lean beef mince**
- **4 red peppers, de-seeded and chopped finely**
- **450 g (1 lb) mushrooms, sliced**
- **1 small red chilli, de-seeded and chopped finely or 1 teaspoon dried chilli flakes**
- **1 kg (2 lb 4 oz) carrots, chopped finely**
- **2 tablespoons dried oregano**
- **1 teaspoon paprika**
- **2 bay leaves**
- **1 tablespoon fennel seeds**
- **1 teaspoon ground cinnamon**
- **2 x 400 g cans of chopped tomatoes**
- **2 tablespoons tomato purée**
- **1 tablespoon Worcestershire sauce**
- **2 x 400 g cans of red kidney beans, drained and rinsed**
- **300 ml (½ pint) vegetable stock**
- **salt and freshly ground black pepper**
- **a small bunch of fresh coriander or parsley, chopped, to serve**

- Heat a very large non stick saucepan or casserole, spray with the low fat cooking spray. Stir fry the onion and garlic for 5 minutes, or until softened, adding a little water if necessary.
- Add the mince and stir fry, breaking it up with a wooden spoon, for 10 minutes, until it is browned all over. Season and add all the other ingredients.
- Bring to the boil and then simmer gently with a lid on for 1½ hours, stirring occasionally. Remove the bay leaves. Serve with the coriander or parsley scattered over the top.

Something sweet

If you enjoy desserts, cakes and bakes then there is no need to deprive yourself of them when you are watching your weight. The trick is to enjoy them in moderation and make informed choices. Just by making small adjustments to your choice of ingredients you can create desserts that are just as delicious as the full-fat versions and that won't send your **POINTS** values sky high. This chapter is packed full of scrumptious desserts, cakes and bakes that allow you to enjoy the sweeter side of life and stay in control of your weight.

Black Forest trifle cake (page 189)

[scrumptious]

3½ POINTS VALUE **Summer fruit and white chocolate fool**

A light and delicious fool. The white chocolate is enough to sweeten the fool without having to add more sugar.

ⓥ *7 POINTS values per recipe* takes 15 minutes to prepare + 30 minutes chilling

Serves 2. 140 calories per serving. Freeze ✗

300 g can of summer fruits, drained
25 g (1 oz) white cooking chocolate
100 g (3½ oz) very low fat plain fromage frais
50 g (1¾ oz) fresh raspberries, to decorate

● Purée the summer fruits in a blender, then place in a large bowl.
● Meanwhile, melt the white chocolate in a large heatproof bowl over a small saucepan of simmering water. Add to the fruit purée and blend again. Fold in the fromage frais and pour into serving glasses or bowls. Serve at once or chill and serve later. Decorate with fresh raspberries.

 2 POINTS VALUE **Walnut brownies**

ⓥ *34 POINTS values per recipe* takes 15 minutes to prepare, 25 minutes to bake + 15 minutes cooling

Makes 16 slices. 124 calories per serving. Freeze ✗

175 g (6 oz) self raising flour, sifted
a pinch of salt
2 tablespoons drinking chocolate
50 g (1¾ oz) soft brown sugar
100 g (3½ oz) polyunsaturated margarine, melted
1 tablespoon white wine vinegar
1 teaspoon vanilla essence
50 g (1¾ oz) walnuts, chopped

● Preheat the oven to Gas Mark 4/180°C/fan oven 160°C. Line a 20 cm (8 inch) square tin with non stick baking parchment.
● Place the flour, salt, drinking chocolate and sugar in a large bowl. Stir to combine.
● Add the margarine, vinegar, vanilla, walnuts and 200 ml (7 fl oz) of cold water. Beat well to make sure there are no lumps of flour left.
● Tip into the baking tin and bake for 25 minutes. Leave to cool in the tin for 15 minutes before slicing into 16 squares. Transfer to a wire rack and allow to cool completely before eating.

How to ●●●

melt chocolate.

Place a saucepan of water on the hob and bring to the boil. Reduce the heat until it is gently simmering. Cut the chocolate into chunks and place it in a heatproof bowl. Put the bowl over the saucepan of water so that the base does not touch the water. Let the chocolate melt gently.

Walnut brownies

Chocolate mocha mousse

These **rich, fluffy mousses** look great in espresso cups with crème fraîche with a pinch of cocoa powder.

Ⓨ *13 POINTS values per recipe* takes 30 minutes to prepare + minimum 30 minutes chilling

Serves 4. 147 calories per serving. Freeze ✗

- **50 g (1¾ oz) plain cooking chocolate (preferably 70% cocoa solids), broken into pieces**
- **1 tablespoon instant coffee, dissolved in 2 tablespoons boiling water, or 2 tablespoons very strong real coffee**
- **4 teaspoons golden syrup**
- **2 egg whites**
- **140 g (5 oz) low fat soft cheese, at room temperature**
- **4 teaspoons half fat crème fraîche, to serve**
- **1 teaspoon cocoa powder, to serve**

● Place the chocolate in a large heatproof bowl, with the coffee and golden syrup. Set over a small saucepan of simmering water until the chocolate melts. Stir together and remove from the heat. Allow to cool slightly – about 10 minutes – until warm but not hot.

● In a separate bowl, whisk the egg whites until stiff.

● Whisk the soft cheese and melted chocolate together until smooth. Gently fold in the egg whites.

● Spoon into four serving glasses, espresso cups or pots and refrigerate for at least 30 minutes, until chilled and set. Decorate each mousse with a teaspoon of crème fraîche and a dusting of cocoa powder to serve.

How to ●●●

whisk egg whites.

Use two eggs that have been left at room temperature and a large mixing bowl that is clean and dry. Separate the eggs and put the whites in the bowl, making sure they are completely free of yolk. Use a whisk (either hand held or electric) and beat until the egg whites are stiff and form peaks when lifted.

 Black Forest trifle cake

This recipe is a bit of a cross between a tiramisu and a Black Forest gateau. Needless to say, it is **utterly delicious** but it is also very quick and easy to make, too.

Ⓨ *23½ POINTS values per recipe* takes 25 minutes to prepare + 30 minutes chilling

Serves 6. 259 calories per serving. Freeze ✗

- **24 sponge fingers**
- **2 x 400 g cans of stoned cherries, drained, 6 tablespoons of juice reserved**
- **2 tablespoons kirsch or brandy (optional)**
- **200 g (7 oz) very low fat fromage frais**
- **150 g (5½ oz) quark**
- **50 g (1¾ oz) icing sugar**
- **1 teaspoon vanilla essence**
- **1 teaspoon cocoa powder, to dust**

● Line the base and sides of a 900 g (2 lb) loaf tin with clingfilm, allowing extra to hang over the sides. Place a layer of eight sponge fingers in the bottom, sugar side down, and then arrange half the cherries on top and sprinkle with half the reserved cherry juice and 1 tablespoon of the kirsch or brandy, if using.

● Beat half of the fromage frais with the Quark, sugar and vanilla essence until smooth. Spread half of this mixture over the cherries. Then arrange another layer of sponge fingers on top. Repeat with the remaining cherries, juice and cheese mixture, finishing with a layer of sponge fingers.

● Fold the clingfilm over the top and press down with your fingers; then chill for at least 30 minutes.

● Turn out on to a serving plate and remove the clingfilm. Spread the top with the remaining fromage frais and dust with cocoa powder.

Passionate pavlova

This meringue based dessert makes a big, bold and beautiful **party extravaganza** to be proud of.

Ⓨ *19 POINTS values per recipe* takes 20 minutes to prepare, 1 hour to bake + 2–3 hours cooling

Serves 6. 220 calories per serving. Freeze ✗

- **4 egg whites**
- **150 g (5½ oz) caster sugar**
- For the topping
- **100 g (3½ oz) quark**
- **400 ml (14 fl oz) very low fat fromage frais**
- **50 g (1¾ oz) icing sugar, with extra to dust**
- **4 passion fruits, seeds and juice scooped out of the shells**
- **2 ripe nectarines, stoned and cut in wedges**
- **450 g (1 lb) strawberries, hulled and sliced**
- **1 teaspoon icing sugar, to decorate**

● Preheat the oven to Gas Mark ½/130°C/fan oven 110°C. With an electric whisk, whisk the egg whites until they are stiff and dry. Whisk in half the sugar, then add the other half and whisk again until stiff and glossy.

● Line a baking sheet with non stick baking parchment, put a 20 cm (8 inch) dinner plate on top and draw round it. Spoon in the meringue to cover the circle, building up the edge and swirling the meringue to make a large, slightly concave nest.

● Bake for 1 hour. Leave to cool in the oven with the door slightly ajar for 2–3 hours.

● Carefully peel off the paper and place on a serving dish.

● To decorate, beat together the quark, fromage frais and icing sugar and spoon on to the pavlova. Top with the fruit and dust with icing sugar to serve.

 Raspberry tart

A **light but sophisticated tart** that makes a perfect summer dessert for a family lunch or dinner with friends.

Ⓨ *13 POINTS values per recipe* takes 40 minutes to prepare + 20 minutes chilling

Serves 6. 118 calories per serving. Freeze ✗

- For the pastry
- **50 g (1¾ oz) polyunsaturated margarine, chilled**
- **75 g (2¾ oz) plain flour**
- **a pinch of sugar**
- For the filling
- **200 g (7 oz) fresh raspberries**
- **4 teaspoons reduced sugar, high fruit content raspberry jam**

● Make the pastry by rubbing the margarine into the flour and sugar in a mixing bowl, until the mixture resembles fresh breadcrumbs; then add 1–2 tablespoons of cold water and bring together quickly with your hand into a ball. Wrap in clingfilm and chill for 20 minutes.

● Preheat the oven to Gas Mark 6/200°C/fan oven 180°C. Roll out the pastry straight on to and slightly bigger than the base of a 19 cm (7½ inch) loose bottomed flan or cake tin. Place the base back into the ring, so that the pastry edge comes slightly up the sides. Push into the corners with your fingers and up at the edge. Line with foil or baking paper and fill with baking beans.

● Bake blind for 10 minutes. Then remove the beans and lining and bake for a further 10 minutes or until evenly golden brown.

● Allow the pastry to cool, then arrange the raspberries on top.

● Heat the jam in a small saucepan with 4–5 teaspoons of water and brush over the raspberries to glaze.

Raspberry and apple cake

This cake is delicious served **warm or cool**, either on its own or with 1 tablespoon of very low fat fromage frais for an extra **POINTS** value of ¹/₂ per serving.

44¹/₂ **POINTS** *values per recipe* takes 20 minutes to prepare, 1–1¹/₄ hours to bake + cooling

Serves 12. 221 calories per serving. Freeze ✗

low fat cooking spray
225 g (8 oz) self raising flour
a pinch of salt
150 g (5¹/₂ oz) polyunsaturated margarine
75 g (2³/₄ oz) caster sugar
225 g (8 oz) eating apples, peeled, cored and chopped
2 eggs, beaten
3 tablespoons skimmed milk
225 g (8 oz) fresh or frozen raspberries
25 g (1 oz) flaked almonds
1 teaspoon icing sugar, to decorate

● Preheat the oven to Gas Mark 4/180°C/fan oven 160°C. Spray a 20 cm (8 inch) round springform cake tin with low fat cooking spray and line it with non stick baking parchment.

● Sift the flour and salt into a large bowl. Rub in the margarine until the mixture resembles fresh breadcrumbs. Stir in the sugar and apples, beat in the eggs and milk. Finally, gently fold in half the raspberries.

● Spoon the mixture into the tin and level the surface; then sprinkle over the remaining raspberries and the flaked almonds. Bake for 1–1¹/₄ hours or until well risen, golden brown and firm to the touch in the centre.

● Remove from the tin and cool on a rack, then dust with icing sugar to serve.

 Chocolate orange cheesecake

29 **POINTS** *values per recipe* takes 55 minutes to bake + 2–3 hours cooling

Serves 10. 162 calories per serving. Freeze ❄

50 g (1³/₄ oz) polyunsaturated margarine, chilled
75 g (2³/₄ oz) plain flour, sifted with a pinch of sugar, plus extra for kneading
low fat cooking spray
For the filling
50 g (1³/₄ oz) plain chocolate, (70% cocoa solids)
250 g (9 oz) very low fat soft cheese, at room temperature
50 g (1³/₄ oz) icing sugar plus 1 teaspoon for dusting
1 tablespoon cornflour
grated zest of 1 orange
2 eggs

● To make the pastry: in a mixing bowl, rub the cold margarine into the flour until it resembles breadcrumbs; then gradually add 2 teaspoons of cold water until the mixture starts to hold together. Turn on to a floured board and knead into a ball. Put in a plastic bag and refrigerate for 30 minutes.

● Preheat the oven to Gas Mark 4/180°C/fan oven 160°C. Remove the base from a loose bottomed 18 cm (7 inch) cake tin, spray with the low fat cooking spray and then place on a work surface.

● Roll and push out the pastry straight on to the base until it is about 5 mm (¹/₄ inch) thick, then reassemble the tin. Cover with foil and scatter with baking beans. Bake for 15 minutes, then remove the foil and baking beans, and put back in the oven for 5 minutes.

● Meanwhile, make the filling. Melt the chocolate in a heatproof bowl over a small saucepan of simmering water, being careful not to let the water touch the bottom of the bowl. Beat together the cheese, sugar, cornflour, orange zest and melted chocolate until well blended; then whisk in the eggs.

● Pour into the tin. Bake for 35 minutes or until just set. Leave the cheesecake to cool and then turn out and serve.

Autumn pudding

Like summer pudding, Autumn pudding is a traditional English pudding that never fails to **excite the taste buds**. Serve with half fat crème fraîche at a *POINTS* value of 1¹/₂ per tablespoonful.

Ⓥ *19¹/₂ POINTS values per recipe* takes 25 minutes + overnight chilling

Serves 6. 195 calories per serving. Freeze ✗

> 2 x 500 g bags of frozen Fruits of the Forest, defrosted, or
>   1 kg (2 lb 4 oz) fresh autumn fruits (e.g. blackberries,
>   late raspberries and elderberries)
> 100 g (3¹/₂ oz) caster sugar
> 8 slices of white bread, crusts removed
> 2 teaspoons rose water (optional)

● Place the fruits in a saucepan with the sugar and cook gently for 10–15 minutes or until just tender.

● Cut one circle of bread for the bottom of a 850 ml (1¹/₂ pint) pudding basin and one for the top.

● Arrange bread slices around the inside of the bowl so that the bowl is completely covered. It does not matter if the bread overlaps but bear in mind what it will look like when the pudding is turned out.

● Pour in the fruit, reserving a spoonful for decorating, and then sprinkle over the rose water, if using, and put the other circle of bread on the top to cover the filling. Cover with a saucer that's small enough to rest inside the bowl, put it in the fridge and weigh it down by placing something heavy on the saucer. Leave overnight.

● Remove the weight and saucer and turn out the pudding on a serving plate. Decorate with reserved fruit.

 ### Christmas pudding with brandy sauce

Ⓥ *47 POINTS values per recipe* takes 45 minutes to prepare, 4¹/₂ hours to cook

Serves 10. 318 calories per serving. Freeze ✗

> low fat cooking spray
> 100 g (3¹/₂ oz) plain flour
> 1 teaspoon baking powder
> 100 g (3¹/₂ oz) low fat margarine
> 100 g (3¹/₂ oz) each of raisins; sultanas; currants; dried apricots,
>   chopped
> 100 g (3¹/₂ oz) caster sugar
> 100 g (3¹/₂ oz) fresh breadcrumbs
> 1 teaspoon each of ground cinnamon; ground ginger;
>   ground cloves; grated nutmeg
> 1 egg
> 150 ml (¹/₂ pint) skimmed milk
> 2 tablespoons brandy
> For the brandy sauce
> 40 g (1¹/₂ oz) cornflour
> 50 g (1³/₄ oz) dark brown sugar
> 600 ml (1 pint) skimmed milk
> 2 tablespoons brandy

● Spray a 1.2 litre (2 pint) pudding basin with the low fat cooking spray and line the base with a disc of non stick baking parchment. Sift the flour and baking powder into a bowl, add the margarine and rub in with your fingertips.

● Stir in the dried fruit, sugar, breadcrumbs and spices. Mix in the egg, milk and brandy. Spoon into the basin and level.

● Cover with a double thickness of greaseproof paper with a pleat in the middle to allow for rising. Fold under the rim. Place in a steamer for 3 hours, checking the water level. The pudding can be kept in the fridge for 3 weeks. Steam for 1¹/₂ hours before serving.

● To make the sauce, blend the cornflour with the sugar and a little of the milk in a saucepan. Add the rest of the milk and bring to the boil, stirring. Cook for 2 minutes, still stirring, until thickened, then add the brandy. Serve with the pudding.

Snow covered Christmas Cake

This traditional Christmas cake makes a **beautiful centrepiece** for your Christmas tea.

105¹/₂ POINTS values per recipe takes 30 minutes to prepare + overnight soaking, 2¹/₂ hours to bake + setting

Serves 18. 373 calories per serving. Freeze ❄ without icing (ice when defrosted)

low fat cooking spray
550 g (1 lb 2¹/₂ oz) dried luxury mixed fruit
100 g (3¹/₂ oz) glacé cherries, halved
100 g (3¹/₂ oz) chopped mixed nuts
juice and finely grated zest of 1 orange
3 tablespoons brandy (or use more orange juice)
225 g (8 oz) polyunsaturated margarine
200 g (7 oz) soft brown sugar
5 eggs
250 g (9 oz) plain flour
2 teaspoons ground mixed spice or cinnamon
For the icing
2 tablespoons low calorie apricot jam
75 g (2³/₄ oz) icing sugar, sifted

● Mix the first five ingredients together in a bowl and leave, preferably overnight, to soak.

● Preheat the oven to Gas Mark 2/150°C/fan oven 130°C. Spray a 21 x 9 cm (8¹/₂ x 3¹/₂ inch) ring tin or a 20 cm (8 inch) round cake tin with the low fat cooking spray.

● Cream the margarine and sugar together until light and fluffy, preferably with an electric whisk. Then beat in the eggs one at a time.

● Sift the flour and mixed spice and lightly fold into the mixture. Then fold in the fruit mixture and make a batter just moist enough to drop off the spoon.

● Spoon into the prepared tin and tie a double layer of baking parchment around it. Bake for about 2¹/₄ hours or until a warm skewer inserted into the middle comes out clean. Cover the cake in the last hour if it is becoming too brown.

● Allow the cake to cool in the tin for an hour before placing on a cooling rack. To keep, wrap in greaseproof paper and then a layer of foil.

● To ice, place the cooled cake on a board and warm the jam in a saucepan with 2 tablespoons of water until melted. Brush the cake with the jam.

● Mix the icing sugar with just enough boiling water to make a smooth, slightly runny mixture (about 2 tablespoons). Drizzle over the top of the cake, allowing it to run down the sides, and then leave to set.

How to ●●●

keep the cake moist.

To stop the cake becoming dry in the run up to Christmas, unwrap it every 1–2 weeks, prick it with a fine skewer and spoon 1 tablespoon of brandy over it.

(2 POINTS VALUE) **Roasted fruits with passion fruit and orange sauce**

A delicious way to serve fruit – the roasting not only softens it but also **draws out the flavours**.

ⓨ *8 POINTS values per recipe* takes 45 minutes

Serves 4. 183 calories per serving. Freeze ✗

- **200 g (7 oz) large strawberries, hulled**
- **2 kiwi fruits, peeled and quartered**
- **1 medium mango, peeled and sliced thickly**
- **4 peaches, quartered**
- **1/2 teaspoon ground cinnamon**
- **juice and zest of 1 orange zest**
- **4 passion fruit**
- **200 g low fat plain yogurt, to serve**

- Preheat the oven to Gas Mark 7/220°C/fan oven 200°C.
- Place the first four fruits into a bowl and sprinkle with the ground cinnamon and orange zest, then mix gently.
- Pour the fruits into a roasting tray and roast for 30 minutes, turning them gently after 15 minutes.
- Place the orange juice in a pan with the juice of the passion fruit – the pips can be sieved out if you wish but it is not necessary. Simmer on a medium heat for 15 minutes until the liquid has reduced slightly.
- Serve the roasted fruits with the passion fruit sauce and the low fat yogurt.

(3 POINTS VALUE) **Mango and lime parfaits**

These parfaits are **simple and quick** to make and pretty enough to serve to guests.

ⓨ *12 1/2 POINTS values per recipe* takes 10 minutes

Serves 4. 203 calories per serving. Freeze ✗

- **200 ml (7 fl oz) mango sorbet**
- **400 g (14 oz) canned mango slices, drained and pureéd in a food processor or blender**
- **200 ml (7 fl oz) lime or lemon sorbet**
- **100 g (3 1/2 oz) blueberries**
- **2 tablespoons very low fat fromage frais**
- **4 fresh mint sprigs**

- Place 1 scoop of mango sorbet in each of four dessert or wine glasses. Top each with some of the mango purée, and a scoop of lime or lemon sorbet.
- Add some blueberries and a half tablespoon of fromage frais. Decorate with the remaining blueberries and mint.

How to ●●●

make your own sorbet.

Purée 350 g (12 oz) of mango and pour this into a measuring jug. Add 6 tablespoons of caster sugar then place the purée in a small pan and heat until boiling. Simmer for a few minutes, with a little water, until the mixture is reduced and thickened. Leave it to cool. Whisk the egg white until stiff then gently fold it into the cool mango mixture. Pour it into a freezer container and freeze for an hour. Stir to break up any lumps.

Mango and lime parfaits

$3\frac{1}{2}$ POINTS VALUE Banana and strawberry cheesecake

This is a **great pudding to share** – creamy cheesecake and fresh fruit.

Ⓥ *35 POINTS values per recipe* takes 20 minutes to prepare, + cooling, 1½–2 hours

Serves 10. 226 calories per serving. Freeze ✗

100 g (3½ oz) caramel rice cakes

4 bananas

juice and zest of 2 lemons

600 g (1 lb 5 oz) low fat soft cheese

1½ tablespoons sweetener

3 tablespoons low fat fromage frais

6 eggs

500 g (1 lb 2 oz) strawberries, sliced

● Preheat the oven to Gas Mark 2/150°C/fan oven 130°C.
● Place the rice cakes in a food processor and process until crumbly.
● Mash the bananas with the lemon juice and mix in the rice cake crumbs.
● Press the mixture into the base of a 23 cm (9 inch) loose-bottomed tin.
● Blend the low fat soft cheese, sweetener and fromage frais together until smooth. Add the eggs and lemon zest and blend again to mix thoroughly.
● Pour the soft cheese mixture over the base and bake in the oven for 1–1½ hours until set.
● Leave to cool in the tin.
● Remove from the tin and decorate with strawberry slices before serving.

Banana and strawberry cheesecake

3 POINTS VALUE Vanilla rice pudding

This **creamy rice pudding** is delicious served hot on its own. Soya milk, now sold widely, is made from yellow soya beans. It has quite a strong flavour and adds a creaminess to recipes such as this. You can use skimmed milk if you prefer, but you will lose some of the creaminess and taste.

Ⓥ *11½ POINTS values per recipe* preparation and cooking time 20–25 minutes

Serves 4. 189 calories per serving. Freeze ✗

700 ml (1¼ pints) soya milk

1 vanilla pod, split and scraped

low fat cooking spray

150 g (5½ oz) risotto rice

1½ tablespoons artificial sweetener

● Place the milk and vanilla pod into a small saucepan and place over a medium heat.
● Spray a medium pan with low fat cooking spray and stir in the rice. Cook over a medium heat whilst stirring, for 2–3 minutes.
● Pour a ladle of the milk into the rice and, with the heat slightly higher so the milk bubbles constantly, stir until all the milk is absorbed. Sprinkle in a little of the sweetener with every addition of milk.
● Keep repeating this process until all the milk is absorbed and you are left with a creamy vanilla rice pudding.

Raspberry meringue frozen yogurt

Ⓨ *7 POINTS values per recipe* takes 15 minutes to prepare + cooling (preferably overnight) + freezing + softening, 1 hour to cook

Serves 4. 70 calories per serving. Freeze ❄

> **3 egg whites**
> **4¹⁄₂ tablespoons artificial sweetener**
> **150 g (5¹⁄₂ oz) raspberries**
> **450 g (1 lb) low fat plain or raspberry yogurt**

- Preheat the oven to Gas Mark 3/170°C/fan oven 150°C.
- Place the egg whites in a completely clean, grease free bowl and whisk until stiff.
- Gradually whisk in the sweetener, 1 tablespoon at a time, until you have a stiff meringue mixture.
- Spoon the mixture on to a greaseproof lined baking sheet in a circle.
- Reduce the oven temperature to Gas Mark 1/140°C/fan oven 120°C and bake for 1 hour.
- Turn off the oven and leave the meringue inside until the oven has cooled (baking meringue just before you go to bed is a good idea, then it can be left in the oven overnight).
- In a large bowl break up the meringue into large pieces. Very carefully mix in the raspberries and yogurt. Spoon into a freezer proof container and freeze.
- Allow time to soften when serving – remove from the freezer about 20 minutes before.

Orange and mango fool

Ⓨ *5¹⁄₂ POINTS values per recipe* takes 10 minutes + 30 minutes chilling

Serves 4. 64 calories per serving. Freeze ✗

> **1 mango, peeled, stoned and chopped**
> **grated zest of 1 orange**
> **100 g (3¹⁄₂ oz) low fat fromage frais**
> **200 g (7 oz) low fat plain yogurt**
> **juice of ¹⁄₂ a lime**

- Place the mango in a food processor or blender and blend until smooth. Pour into a bowl.
- Whisk in the remaining ingredients; then pour into four glasses and chill for 30 minutes before serving.

Apricot mousse

 5 POINTS values per recipe takes 10 minutes + 20 minutes chilling
Serves 4. 80 calories per serving. Freeze ✗

150 ml (¼ pint) boiling water

1 sachet of sugar free jelly – flavour of your choice

410 g can of apricots in juice

200 g (7 oz) low fat apricot or plain yogurt

● Pour the boiling water into a measuring jug. Sprinkle over the sugar free jelly powder and stir until dissolved. Leave to cool slightly.

● Drain the apricots and, reserving one half of them for decoration, blend the rest in a food processor until smooth.

● Whisk together the apricot purée and yogurt.

● When the jelly is only warm, whisk it into the yogurt mixture.

● Place in the fridge for 20 minutes.

● Take out and whisk again and divide between four glasses or small bowls.

● Chill until ready to serve. Slice the remaining apricots in half and use them to decorate the mousses.

Apple and pear sorbet

 6 POINTS values per recipe takes 35 minutes to prepare + cooling + 2 hours freezing
Serves 4. 111 calories per serving. Freeze ❄

4 ripe dessert apples, peeled and cored

4 ripe pears, peeled and cored

juice of 1 lemon

½ teaspoon cinnamon powder

● Place the fruit in a medium pan. Pour in enough water just to cover the base of the pan. Simmer for 15–20 minutes or until the fruit is soft. Leave to cool.

● Place the cooled fruit in a blender or food processor with the lemon juice and cinnamon powder. Process until nearly smooth.

● Place the sorbet mixture into an ice cream maker and churn until frozen. (if you do not have one, place in a freezer proof container and freeze. After 2 hours take out and whisk up with a fork and return to the freezer).

● Always allow time for the sorbet to soften before serving – take out of the freezer at least 20 minutes before serving.

Cinnamon peach compôte

This is a **lovely flavoured dessert**, which tastes great with the Vanilla Rice Pudding (page 199).

2 POINTS values per recipe takes 15 minutes + cooling

Serves 4. 59 calories per serving. Freeze ✗

4 peaches, stoned and cut into quarters

1 stick of lemon grass, bruised

2 cm (³/4 inch) fresh root ginger, sliced

1 cinnamon stick

1 teaspoon artificial sweetener

● Place all the ingredients in a pan and just cover with water.

● Bring to the boil and then simmer for 8–10 minutes depending on the ripeness of the fruit. Leave to cool in the syrup then serve.

Mango, raspberry and blueberry pavlova

11 POINTS values per recipe takes 15 minutes to prepare, 1 hour to bake

Serves 4–6. 139 calories per serving. Freeze ✗

3 egg whites

4¹/2 tablespoons artificial sweetener

450 g (1 lb) low fat raspberry yogurt

150 g (5¹/2 oz) raspberries

125 g (4¹/2 oz) blueberries

2 mangoes, stoned, peeled and sliced

● Preheat the oven to Gas Mark 3/170°C/fan oven 150°C.

● Place the egg whites in a completely clean, grease free bowl and whisk until stiff.

● Gradually whisk in the sweetener, one tablespoon at a time, until you have a stiff meringue mixture.

● Spoon the mixture onto a greaseproof lined baking sheet in a circle, with a slight dip in the centre.

● Reduce the oven temperature to Gas Mark 1/140°C/fan oven 120°C and bake for 1 hour.

● Turn off the oven and leave the pavlova inside until the oven has cooled (baking pavlova just before you go to bed is a good idea, then it can be left in the oven overnight).

● When you are ready to serve the pavlova, gently remove the greaseproof paper and place on a serving plate.

● Spoon over the yogurt and top with the fruits. Serve immediately.

How to ●●●

bruise lemon grass.

Cut the trimmed stalk at a very sharp angle into 2.5 cm (1 inch) long pieces, exposing the fragrant interior. Then smash, with a flat blade, cleaver or heavy knife, to release the aromatic oils before adding it to the other ingredients.

Index by *POINTS* values